EFFECTIVE EXECUTIVE'S

The Seven Steps for Creating High-Value, High-Impact PowerPoint Presentations

GUIDE TO POWERPOINT 2002

EFFECTIVE EXECUTIVE'S

The Seven Steps for Creating High-Value, High-Impact PowerPoint Presentations

GUIDE TO POWERPOINT 2002

Stephen L. Nelson
Michael Buschmohle

REDMOND TECHNOLOGY PRESS

Effective Executive's Guide to PowerPoint 2002:
The Seven Steps for Creating High-Value, High-Impact PowerPoint Presentations

Published by
Redmond Technology Press
8581 154th Avenue NE
Redmond, WA 98052
www.redtechpress.com

Library of Congress Catalog Card No: applied for

ISBN 1-931150-00-1
Printed and bound in the United States of America.

9 8 7 6 5 4 3 2 1

Distributed by
Independent Publishers Group
814 N. Franklin St.
Chicago, IL 60610
www.ipgbook.com

Product and company names mentioned herein may be the trademarks of their respective owners.

To the family I grew up with in Michigan and the family still teaching me to grow up in Washington: Charlotte, Zac, and Marissa. MB

To Sue, Beth, and Britt—thanks for cheerfully letting me disappear for the month of mornings it took to write my part of this book. SN

Acknowledgments

Special thanks to our project editors, Becky Whitney and Paula Thurman, and our technical editor, Anne Sandbo.

Contents at a Glance

Contents

Step 3   **Add Objects**   **41**

Step 4   Design Your Look   73

Step 5   Add Special Effects   97

Step 6   **Prepare Your Presentation**   **117**

Appendix B **Using WordArt** **181**

INTRODUCTION

You've just been invited to deliver an important presentation. The conference room will be filled with clients, shareholders, and key officials, and you want this presentation to be the best you've ever given.

Where do you begin? One place to begin is with Microsoft PowerPoint. This amazing software can make you look like a genius . . . and even earn you an occasional standing ovation. When it comes to giving presentations, in fact, PowerPoint can be your best friend from start to finish . . .

. . . which is maybe why you're reading this book or considering this book. However, one problem with many books about PowerPoint is this: They're only about PowerPoint.

In comparison, we've written this book to help you deliver outstanding presentations. We assume that you don't need to become an expert authority in using PowerPoint. You just want to be knowledgeable enough to produce effective presentations with slides and handouts. You'll learn plenty about using commands, dialog box buttons, and animation features; PowerPoint has more capabilities than most executives will probably ever use. Our focus will be on you and your desire to give presentations that get your ideas across, satisfy the information needs of your listeners, and earn you the respect and recognition you deserve.

This *Effective Executive's Guide* does not try to be an encyclopedic manual. Instead, it focuses on the process of creating a presentation in seven distinct steps. We think that this logical seven-step approach works best for typical PowerPoint users: executives and business professionals. Breaking the process into steps gives you a book that filters everything we *could* say about PowerPoint into just what most executive users *should* know.

What This Book Assumes About You

This book makes two assumptions about you. First, you're not and don't want to become a PowerPoint expert. Rather, we assume that you're a professional working in business, a nonprofit organization, or public service. And we assume that you want to use PowerPoint to enhance the presentations you make.

The book also assumes that you're familiar working with the Microsoft Windows operating system. As a result, in the pages that follow you won't get detailed information about how to choose menu commands or select dialog box buttons and boxes. If you don't already possess this knowledge, you'll need to acquire it by either using the online help available in Windows, getting a quick tutorial from someone like a co-worker, or reading a good introductory book on Windows.

How This Book Is Organized

As noted, this book breaks the process of using PowerPoint to create a presentation into seven steps. Each step gets described in its own chapter. These chapters, or steps, are described here.

Step 1: Learn the Logic

The place to start any discussion of using PowerPoint is with information about what the PowerPoint program does and the terms it uses. In Step 1, we provide this information.

Step 2: Outline Your Content

After you understand how PowerPoint works, your next step is to create a textual list, or *outline,* of the messages and points you want to share. Typically, you'll do this using the PowerPoint program, but you can also work in another program, like Microsoft Word, and then export your outline to PowerPoint.

Step 3: Add Objects

After you outline your content, almost always you'll want to create objects you can add to your presentation. *Objects* are tables, charts, and pictures that augment the textual information in your outline. You can create a rich variety of useful objects using the PowerPoint program. You can also create objects using other programs (such as those that make up Microsoft Office).

Step 4: Design Your Look

After you've outlined your content and created any objects, you move past the substance of your presentation and address its form, its appearance, and its "look." One of the big benefits of using PowerPoint is that it lets you easily create a presentation that looks professional using built-in tools and features like design templates and color schemes.

Step 5: Add Special Effects

You need to be judicious in adding special effects like slide transitions, animation, sound, and video. But these garnishments can, with common sense, enhance your presentation's impact and value.

Step 6: Prepare Your Presentation

After you've created your presentation, you need to prepare for delivering it by creating speaker's notes, rehearsing, producing any handouts, and tailoring your presentation's slides for the presentation method. Note that PowerPoint provides a rich set of alternative methods for making presentations, including an onscreen display, the use of color projectors and 35mm slides, and the World Wide Web.

Step 7: Deliver Your Presentation

The final step is the successful delivery of your presentation. Although this step represents the culmination of your work, it's actually the easiest in terms of PowerPoint mechanics.

NOTE *In addition to the seven steps, or chapters, described in the preceding paragraphs, this book includes three appendixes and a glossary of PowerPoint and presentation terms: Appendix A, "Creating Better Charts with Microsoft Graph," discusses some fundamentals of good chart design, strengths and weaknesses of chart types, and avoiding common charting mistakes. Appendix B, "Using WordArt" explains how to use the WordArt program to turn text into graphical objects. (The Graph and WordArt programs come with the PowerPoint program.) Appendix C, "Customizing PowerPoint," describes options to customize the setup of your PowerPoint program.*

Conventions Used in This Book

This book uses three conventions worth mentioning here. First, we view this book as a conversation among professionals. This statement means that the pronoun *we* refers to us, the authors. And it means that the pronoun *you* refers to you, the reader. In this case, this conversational style means that you will frequently see the *we* pronoun because two of us, Buschmohle and Nelson, wrote the book. Although *we* has sometimes been used as a stilted, almost royal, self-reference by writers, please don't take it that way. Think of us as workshop presenters or discussion group facilitators, with jackets off and ties loosened. Think of us, in other words, as colleagues. Think of this book as a conversation.

Another convention is that we call the main chapters of the book "steps." The benefit of doing this is that it lets us focus on and emphasize the process of creating a presentation. But, unfortunately, there's a slight problem with this convention. We also want to provide numbered step-by-step instructions in the chapters, or steps, of the book. Whenever some task can't be described in a sentence or two, in fact, we'll use numbered steps to make sure that you can follow the discussion. So this "chapters-that-we-call-steps" convention may confuse matters. If we say, "In the preceding step, we described how to do such-and-such," are we referring to the preceding chapter or to a preceding numbered step? You see the difficulty.

Here's what we've come up with. Whenever we use the term *step* to refer to a chapter, we'll just give you the entire chapter name. For example, if we say that in "Step 3: Add Objects" we describe how to do such-and-such, you'll know what we mean. If we don't give you the chapter name, you'll know that we're talking about the preceding numbered step.

A third convention concerns references to the buttons and boxes in PowerPoint windows and dialog boxes. This book capitalizes the initial letter of the words that label buttons and boxes, even though they don't appear that way onscreen. For example, the check box that is labeled "Loop continuously until Esc" gets referenced in these pages as the Loop Continuously Until Esc box. The initial caps, then, will be a signal to you that we're referring to a label.

Some Caveats

As a communication tool, PowerPoint follows an ancient tradition. From the earliest cave paintings in France to sketches by Leonardo da Vinci to the crayon drawings of children, people have always sought to present ideas in pictures. With PowerPoint, you have a true tool that matches or replaces last century's most popular business communication media: chalkboards, easel charts, 35mm slides, and overhead transparencies. These older technologies are still used and valuable; it's just that now we have so many more options with computer programs such as PowerPoint.

Nonetheless, before we move into our main discussion about PowerPoint, it's probably useful to issue a caveat or two about using it. Although PowerPoint is rapidly becoming the worldwide standard for business and technical presentations, prudent decisions need to be made about when or whether to use it. Before you rush to prepare a PowerPoint presentation (or take the time to read any of this book), we recommend that you answer three basic but important questions:

- Can PowerPoint slides be shown in the room where you'll be speaking? To use PowerPoint, obviously, adequate equipment needs to be available: a laptop, projector, screen, and cables, for example. Furthermore, and assuming that these prerequisites are met, you want to verify that the room seating and viewing will or can be arranged to accommodate PowerPoint.

- Is PowerPoint appropriate for the kind of presentation you intend to give? It might not be necessary if your aim is strictly interactive participation, group sharing, or discussion. PowerPoint can be used for portions of such meetings when information must be presented, of course. But projecting slides might not work if you meet in a tiny room where PowerPoint will overwhelm listeners. In such cases, you may want to show slides on a monitor or laptop screen or distribute handouts you've created with PowerPoint.

- What is the attitude toward PowerPoint among members of the audience? Many business and professional audiences expect and welcome PowerPoint. A few audiences have already overdosed on the program and complain, "Every presentation looks alike." Check out beforehand whether listeners would welcome or be turned off by PowerPoint, and adjust your presentation so that people are willing to listen. You can help your cause by making sure that *your* PowerPoint slides look better than others the audience has seen. Follow the guidelines in this book, and your slides will stand out.

Step 1

LEARN THE LOGIC

Featuring:
- What Is PowerPoint?
- How PowerPoint Works
- Key PowerPoint Terms
- Approaches for Creating Presentations

Before you even begin working with PowerPoint, you should understand what PowerPoint does and how to use it. You'll also benefit immensely if you understand, from the beginning, some key PowerPoint terms and the three different approaches for creating PowerPoint presentations. In this step, we discuss these key topics and concepts.

What Is PowerPoint?

You can answer the question "What is PowerPoint?" in two useful ways. You can say that PowerPoint is a presentation program. That means, in a nutshell, that it simply helps you create slides, such as the one shown in Figure 1-1.

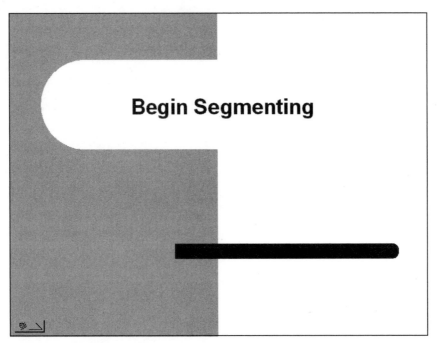

Figure 1-1 A PowerPoint title slide.

Figure 1-1 shows what's called the title slide. But that doesn't actually matter at this point. The main thing to recognize is that this slide—which might be a 35mm slide—is the building block you create with the PowerPoint program.

You can also answer the "What is PowerPoint?" question by saying that PowerPoint is part of the Microsoft Office suite of programs. This fact has two noteworthy ramifications:

- If you know how to use one program in the Office suite—such as Microsoft Word or Microsoft Excel—you already know much of what you need to know about working with PowerPoint. The things you create in PowerPoint—called *documents* or *presentations*—get created in the same basic way as the pages of a Word document and the spreadsheets in an Excel workbook. And the programs in the Microsoft Office suite resemble each other. In fact, many of the menus, commands, toolbar buttons and boxes, and dialog boxes are identical or almost identical. For example, the dialog box you use to name and choose a location for a PowerPoint presentation you save is identical to the dialog box you use to name and specify a location for a Word document or Excel workbook you save.

- Almost anything you build using another Microsoft program can be used in a PowerPoint slide. So, for example, if you create a table or a bulleted list in Word, that information can easily be used on a PowerPoint slide. And, if you create a chart or a small spreadsheet in Excel, again, that information can easily be used in a PowerPoint slide.

How PowerPoint Works

PowerPoint provides tools and prefabricated slides you can use to build a presentation you want to give. The slides in a presentation can look like the one shown in Figure 1-1 and contain only text. But slides in PowerPoint can also easily show other objects, like tables (see Figure 1-2), charts (see Figure 1-3), organizational charts, drawings and pictures, and even clipart.

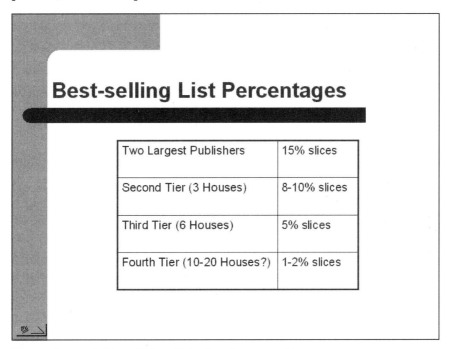

Figure 1-2   A PowerPoint slide that shows a table.

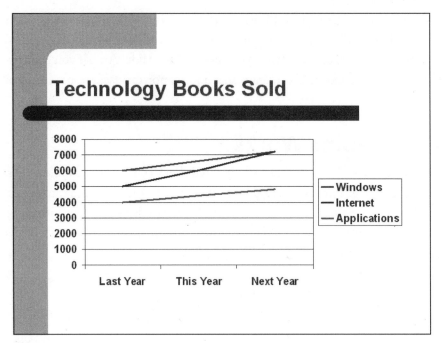

Figure 1-3   A PowerPoint slide that shows a chart.

The other thing to note about PowerPoint is that it not only helps you create the slides (such as those shown in Figures 1-1, 1-2, and 1-3), but it also provides tools you can use to present your slides. For example, PowerPoint includes a wizard you can use to create the raw files you need to send to a film company when you want to create 35mm slides. PowerPoint includes tools you can employ to create color transparencies and printed handouts. And PowerPoint includes features that let you easily show the slides you've created onscreen (such as on a laptop) or using a color projector (such as for larger audience presentations).

NOTE   Wizards *are little programs that use dialog boxes to collect information from you and then use the information to perform some task. If you have ever worked with Microsoft Excel and created a chart, for example, you have encountered the Excel Chart Wizard. It asks you questions about the data you want to use in a chart, and then it creates the chart for you.*

Key PowerPoint Terms

PowerPoint, as mentioned earlier, is not a difficult program to use. What it helps you do is actually very simple. Nevertheless, you will benefit from the very start by understanding several key terms.

Slide

A *slide* is the basic building block you create using PowerPoint. The elements you see in Figures 1-1, 1-2, and 1-3 are slides. If you were giving a slide show using, for example, a 35mm slide projector and you created your slides using PowerPoint, what you see in these figures would be what you display on a screen or wall.

Presentation

A *presentation* consists of the slides you've created to show all at the same time. For example, the slides in Figures 1-1, 1-2, and 1-3 might be a presentation.

A presentation is also, from the PowerPoint perspective, a document file. What is stored on your hard disk or on a removable disk, like a floppy disk or zip disk, is actually the presentation file.

If you've worked with Microsoft Word or any other word processing program, you can think of the relationship between a presentation and a slide in the same way you think of a document and a page. A *document,* such as a report you create using Word, consists of individual pages that combine to make the complete document. The individual pages of the report are stored in the document. PowerPoint slides combine to make the complete presentation, which is actually stored in a presentation file.

Text

Text, of course, is simply text. It represents the basic building block and the most common element you'll use on your slides. The slide shown in Figure 1-1, for example, simply uses text to introduce the presentation to the audience. Figure 1-2 showed a table, which is simply a grid of rows and columns, with text in the cells, or squares, of the table.

Text can also appear in a bulleted list, another common format. Figure 1-4 shows a simple slide that uses a bulleted list.

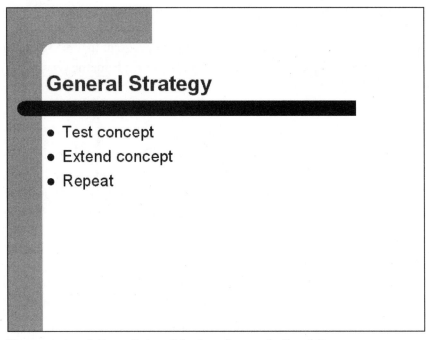
General Strategy

- Test concept
- Extend concept
- Repeat

Figure 1-4   A PowerPoint slide that shows a bulleted list.

NOTE   *You enter and edit text in PowerPoint in the same basic way as you enter and edit text in most other programs. Entering and editing text in PowerPoint, for example, works the same way it does in Microsoft Word.*

Placeholder

In PowerPoint, you enter text and any other items you use for slides into an area of a slide called a *placeholder*. A chunk of text, for example, goes into a text placeholder. A picture, table, or chart also goes into a placeholder.

Placeholders amount to boxes, or areas, that you use to affix things to a slide. You can almost think of them as being like glue. Figure 1-5 shows the PowerPoint program window, which we'll talk about in just a few paragraphs. Note that the window shows a slide with a placeholder for entering a chunk of text to title the slide and another placeholder for entering a bulleted list.

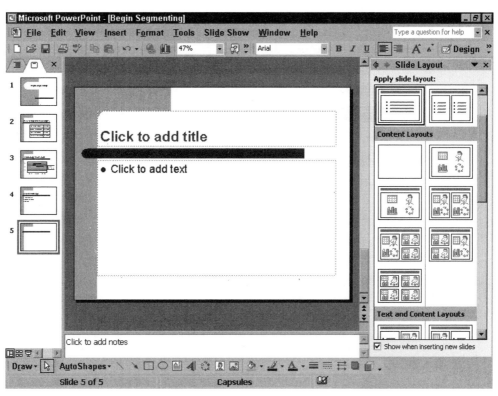

Figure 1-5   A slide with placeholders.

Object

In addition to text, as just mentioned, you can place other items on a slide. PowerPoint calls these items *objects*. For example, the chart shown in Figure 1-3 is an object—a chart object, to be precise. But slides can include a wide variety of objects.

Anything you can create or store on your computer can probably be turned into an object and then placed on a PowerPoint slide. Objects can be chunks of documents you create using other programs, like Microsoft Word or Microsoft Excel; little images or pictures stored as files on your hard disk; or even things like charts, such as organization charts and drawings you create with PowerPoint's many applets.

NOTE   *PowerPoint supplies several small programs, called applets. The applets are essentially miniature programs that are built into the larger PowerPoint program. PowerPoint includes the Microsoft Graph applet, for example, which lets you create charts and graphs. The Microsoft Organization Chart applet, also available from within the PowerPoint program, lets you create organization charts.*

PowerPoint program window

If you've worked with other Microsoft Office programs, the Microsoft PowerPoint *program window* won't surprise you. But just to make sure that you have no questions at the start, let's make a few observations about the window. Figure 1-6 shows a PowerPoint window using the slide from Figure 1-2. There are several things to quickly note about the PowerPoint program window.

NOTE   *Sometimes people also call the program window by another term—application window.*

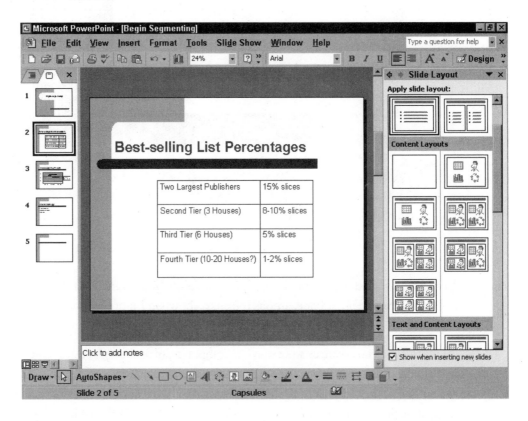

Figure 1-6   The PowerPoint program window with a maximized window.

The program window shows the usual title bar, menu bar, and one or more toolbars. This information appears at the top of the program window.

In the area beneath the menu bar and toolbars, PowerPoint displays a presentation window. PowerPoint uses its presentation window to display the presentation you've opened or are creating. This is the same way that a program like Microsoft Word uses a document window to display the document you are using or creating.

NOTE   *A presentation window is the same thing as a document window.*

PowerPoint uses different panes in the presentation window. The leftmost *Outline pane* lists each of the slides in a presentation. The large center *Slide pane* shows a picture of the active slide you're creating or changing. The smaller *Notes pane* immediately beneath the slide pane provides space for you to record any speaking notes for the displayed slide. Finally, the right most *task pane* displays buttons, command and hyperlinks useful for working with new presentations, designing slides and adding new slides.

NOTE   *To remove a pane, click the pane's close box. To return the PowerPoint window to its usual look of an Outline pane, a Slide pane, a Notes pane and a task pane, choose the View menu's Normal command.*

PowerPoint view

One final term that is useful to understand from the start is *view*. A view is just a way of looking at some of the information in a PowerPoint presentation. One way to look at the information in a PowerPoint presentation is by looking at the slide and nothing else. This is called *Slide Show view*. If you were looking at the slide shown in Figure 1-1 using this view, all you would see is what appears in Figure 1-1. You wouldn't see the PowerPoint program window—only the slide.

PowerPoint also supplies other views. Figure 1-6, for example, shows PowerPoint's Normal view, which is what you often use to create your presentation. Normal view shows the presentation's outline and the slide you are working with inside the PowerPoint program window. Normal view also provides, at the bottom of the presentation window, a small area, or *pane,* that you can use to record speaker's notes and a task pane along the right edge of the window.

Figure 1-7 shows another common view you'll use. The view shown in Figure 1-7 is *Slide Sorter view*. It displays inside the presentation window each of the slides in your presentation. Slide Sorter view (and we will talk about this subject later in this book, in "Step 6: Prepare Your Presentation") lets you rearrange the order of slides and even easily add or delete slides.

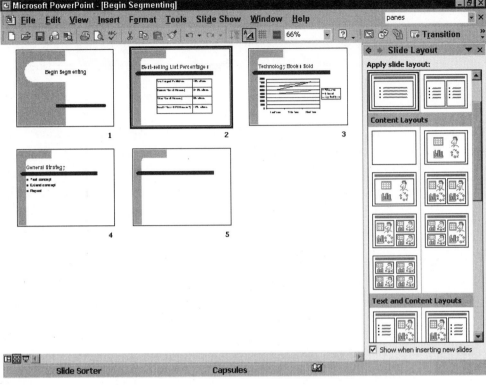

Figure 1-7   Slide Sorter view.

Approaches for Creating Presentations

You can create PowerPoint presentations in three different ways. "Step 2: Outline Your Content" describes this process in more detail, but it is useful to briefly mention and discuss the three ways here.

Using the AutoContent Wizard

The easiest way for new PowerPoint users to create a PowerPoint presentation is by using the AutoContent Wizard. When you start PowerPoint, it first displays the Default Design shown in Figure 1-8.

To use the AutoContent Wizard, you click the From AutoContent Wizard hyperlink in the New Presentation pane, as shown in Figure 1-8.

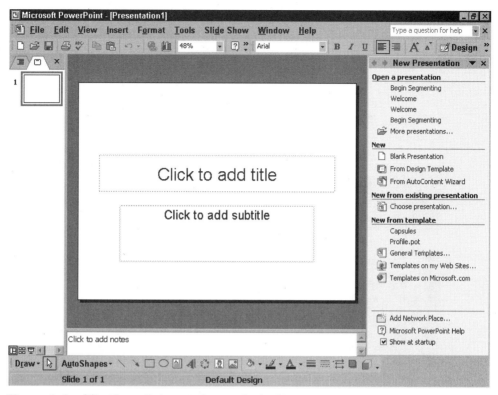

Figure 1-8   The PowerPoint window with the New Presentation pane displayed.

PowerPoint starts the AutoContent Wizard. Figure 1-9 shows the first AutoContent Wizard dialog box.

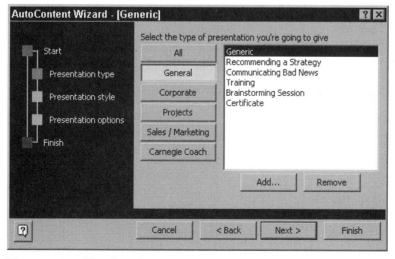

Figure 1-9   The first dialog box displayed by the AutoContent Wizard.

To use the AutoContent Wizard, you simply answer PowerPoint's questions about the presentation you want to create. The first question you'll have to answer, for example, is about the type of presentation you want to give. To identify the type of presentation you want to give, or create, you click one of the buttons in the AutoContent Wizard dialog box, as shown in Figure 1-10: General, Corporate, Projects, Sales/Marketing, or Carnegie Coach. After you've selected a category presentation, you then select one of the specific presentation entries from the List box.

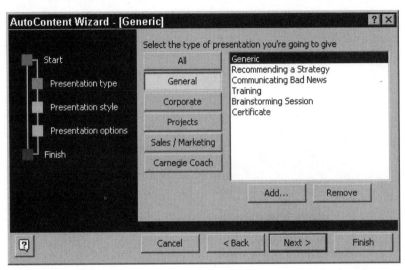

Figure 1-10 The first dialog box displayed by the AutoContent Wizard that asks a question.

In the other dialog boxes the AutoContent Wizard uses, it asks you for additional information about the presentation you are creating. For example, the next AutoContent Wizard dialog box asks how you plan to deliver the presentation, and the third and final dialog box asks you for the name of your presentation and whether there is information you want each of your slides to show.

The AutoContent Wizard can be a wonderful way to create a rough-draft outline for a presentation. And because the AutoContent Wizard suggests good outlines, you might want to review them even when you want to build your own outlines from scratch. But presentations produced by the AutoContent Wizard do tend to resemble each other. And that might be something you want to avoid—especially if you're presenting to audiences that will also see PowerPoint presentations from other (perhaps competitive) speakers on the same subject.

Using an outline

A second method or approach for creating a presentation is by building an outline. An *outline* simply lists the slides in your presentation by slide title. The outline also provides any bulleted text for your slides.

Using an outline is the approach we recommend because it focuses your attention on the content of your presentation and the message you want to deliver. By creating your own outline from scratch, you also are more likely to create a unique presentation—one with unique information and one that's memorable.

Building a presentation with slides

There is a third way to build a presentation: by simply creating individual slides. In other words, you can tell PowerPoint that you want to add a slide to the open presentation and what you want the slide, roughly speaking, to look like. Then you add text and other objects to the slide.

This slide-based method is one that people commonly use. But we suspect that it is also the method from which most bad PowerPoint presentations originate. A slide-based construction method too easily produces presentations that don't make structural sense and instead resemble patchwork quilts of slides. For this reason, this book ignores this third presentation-building approach.

Step 2

OUTLINE YOUR CONTENT

Featuring:

- Using the AutoContent Wizard
- Using Outline View to Create Your Outline
- Reviewing Simple Presentation Strategies
- Importing an Outline
- Working on Your Outline
- Saving and Later Opening Your Outline

After you understand the logic and language of PowerPoint, you're ready to begin building presentations. The first step you take in this construction process is outlining your content. In outlining your content, what you really do is create a list of the slides (and some other information) you want to share.

PowerPoint provides three approaches for creating an outline: You can use the AutoContent Wizard, you can use PowerPoint's Outline view, or you can import an outline from another program—such as an outline you've created in Microsoft Word. All three approaches are discussed in the pages that follow.

Using the AutoContent Wizard

The easiest way for new PowerPoint users to create an outline is by using the AutoContent Wizard. To use the AutoContent Wizard to create your outline, follow these steps:

1. Tell PowerPoint that you want to use the AutoContent Wizard.

As you start the PowerPoint program, it displays the New Presentations task pane shown in Figure 2-1. This pane provides hyperlinks you can use to specify how you want to create the new presentation. To create the presentation using the AutoContent Wizard, you click the From AutoContent Wizard hyperlink. PowerPoint starts the AutoContent Wizard.

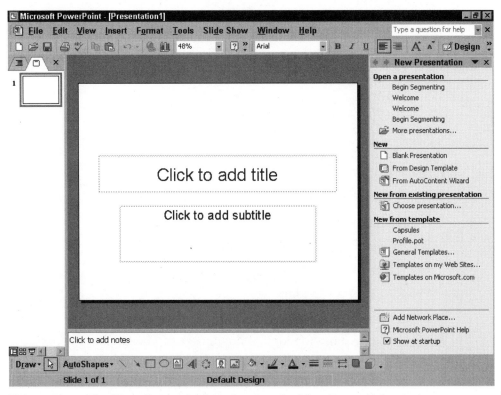

Figure 2-1   The PowerPoint window showing the New Presentation task pane.

If you want to start the AutoContent Wizard after you've already begun creating a presentation's slides, you can redisplay the New Presentations task pane (if necessary) and click the From AutoContent Wizard hyperlink.

TIP   *If the task pane doesn't appear in the PowerPoint window, choose the View menu's Task Pane command. If the task pane appears but doesn't show the New Presentation tasks, use the task pane's Back and Forward buttons.*

2. Begin the AutoContent Wizard.

When you start the AutoContent Wizard, PowerPoint displays an informational dialog box, as shown in Figure 2-2. This dialog box simply introduces the AutoContent Wizard. Click the Next button.

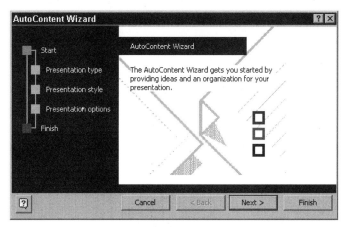

Figure 2-2   The first information dialog box the AutoContent Wizard displays.

3. Select the type of presentation you want to create.

When PowerPoint displays the AutoContent Wizard dialog box shown in Figure 2-3, click the button that best describes the general category of presentation you want to create. This dialog box provides several buttons and category combinations: General, Corporate, Projects, Sales/Marketing, and Carnegie Coach. When you click a button, the AutoContent Wizard displays a list of prefabricated presentations within that category. You select one of these presentations—they're really just partially structured presentations—by clicking it. Click the Next button to continue.

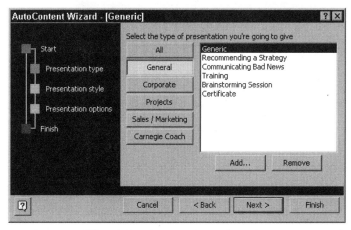

Figure 2-3   The dialog box that the AutoContent Wizard uses to ask you about what type of presentation you want to create.

When you are working with the AutoContent Wizard dialog box shown in Figure 2-3, be sure to explore the presentations in each of the five categories—or at least do this the first few times you use the AutoContent Wizard. The AutoContent Wizard supplies a rich set of thoughtful, well-structured presentations, and—especially as you are starting out—you can benefit by using these presentations as models for your own.

4. Select the presentation style.

When PowerPoint displays the AutoContent Wizard dialog box shown in Figure 2-4, use it to tell the AutoContent Wizard how you'll deliver your presentation. If you will deliver your presentation onscreen using your laptop computer, for example, mark the On-Screen Presentation button. Alternatively, if you are going to publish your presentation to the Web—this could be either an Internet or intranet web site—you mark the Web Presentation button. When you finish providing this information, click the Next button to continue.

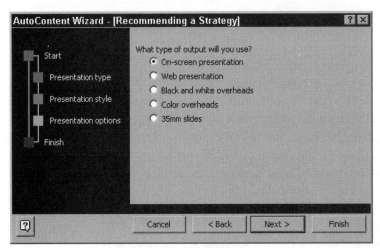

Figure 2-4   The dialog box that the AutoContent Wizard uses to ask you about how you'll share your presentation.

5. Provide general information about the presentation.

When the AutoContent Wizard displays the dialog box shown in Figure 2-5, use the Presentation Title box to name your presentation. Optionally, use the Footer box to provide a footer that will appear at the bottom of each of the slides you create. If you want the footer to include the date the presentation was last modified, or updated, and the number of the slide, mark the Date Last Updated box and the Slide Number box.

NOTE   *You might use the footer to name the presenting organization. You might also use the footer to record a copyright notice or a confidential notice.*

After you've finished filling in the boxes and marking the check boxes provided by the Presentation Options dialog box, click the Next button. Then click the Finish button.

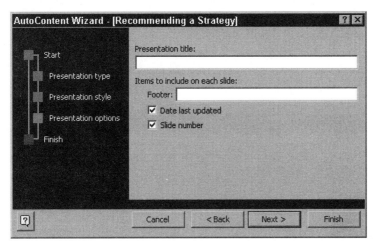

Figure 2-5   The dialog box that the AutoContent Wizard uses to ask you for general information it will place on each slide.

After you click Finish, the AutoContent Wizard creates a rough outline of your presentation and opens the presentation using its Normal view, as shown in Figure 2-6. Normal view includes the outline of the presentation (the outline appears in the pane along the left edge of the PowerPoint program window). Normal view also shows the selected slide in the main pane of the PowerPoint program window. You'll be able to identify the slide because you'll see your presentation title on the slide. If you chose to enter a footer, you'll also see this information at the bottom of the slide.

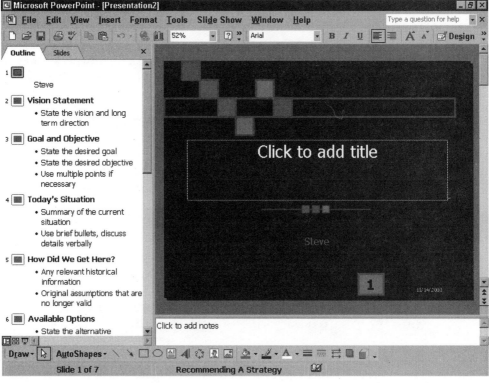

Figure 2-6 Normal view showing an outline created by the AutoContent Wizard.

After you've used the AutoContent Wizard to create a rough-cut outline for your presentation, you next modify the outline so that it matches your presentation requirements. To do this, you'll add slides, add and edit slide text, and probably remove unneeded slides. For information about how to do this, refer to the "Working on Your Outline" section, later in this step.

NOTE *If you are going to use the AutoContent Wizard as described in the preceding list of instructions, you don't need to read the next section, about using Outline view to create your outline, or the section "Importing an Outline," later in this step. You already created your outline. Nevertheless, you might want to skim these sections' information. In the future, you'll probably move to one of these other outline methods.*

Using Outline View to Create Your Outline

If you want to create your own outline from scratch (and avoid the sameness and non-uniqueness that might stem from using the AutoContent Wizard), you use a different approach to create your outline. When PowerPoint displays the New Presentation task pane shown in Figure 2-1, you should click the From Design Template or the Blank Presentation hyperlink. By choosing one of these other creation options, you avoid using the AutoContent Wizard and instead create your own outline from scratch.

Building on a design template

If you choose the From Design Template hyperlink, PowerPoint replaces the New Presentation task pane with the Slide Design task pane, as shown in Figure 2-7. The list box on the Slide Design pane shows examples of more than two dozen predesigned presentation templates you can use to build your presentation. A *presentation template* is really a design or look that will be used for the background of your presentation.

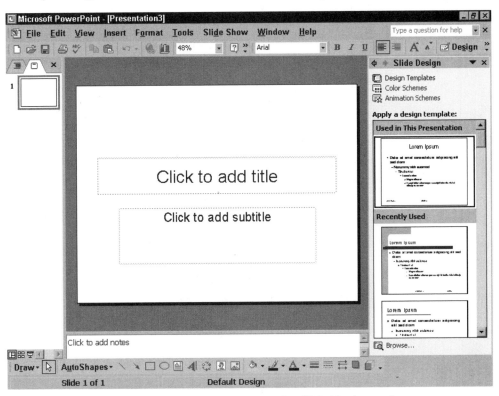

Figure 2-7 The PowerPoint window showing the Slide Design task pane.

NOTE   *The list of design templates shown in the Slide Design task pane includes a button to install additional templates. If you select this button, PowerPoint might ask you to find the Microsoft Office CD or the Microsoft PowerPoint CD. PowerPoint will then use the CD to install the additional design templates.*

Building on a blank presentation

The other way to create your new presentation without using the AutoContent Wizard is simply by clicking the Blank Presentation hyperlink (this hyperlink appears in the New Presentation task pane.) When you click this button, Power Point shows the Slide Layout task pane, as shown in Figure 2-8.

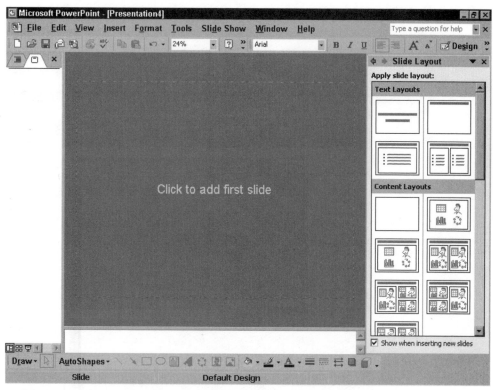

Figure 2-8   The PowerPoint window showing the Slide Layout task pane.

Adding the first slide

If you create an outline based on a design template or blank presentation, you use the Slide Layout task pane to add slides to your presentation.

What you want to do is select the slide layout from the list of slide layouts that are provided.

NOTE   Slide layouts *are simply blank slides that include placeholders for text and other objects. When you select a slide layout, simply pick one that shows the object placeholder or placeholders you want.*

After you select the slide layout for the first slide in your presentation, PowerPoint displays the presentation in Normal view. Figure 2-9 shows how Normal view looks when you are creating your outline based on a blank presentation. The only thing that's different, if you are creating your outline based on a design template, is that the example slide shown in the slide pane of the view will include some design elements, such as color and background graphics.

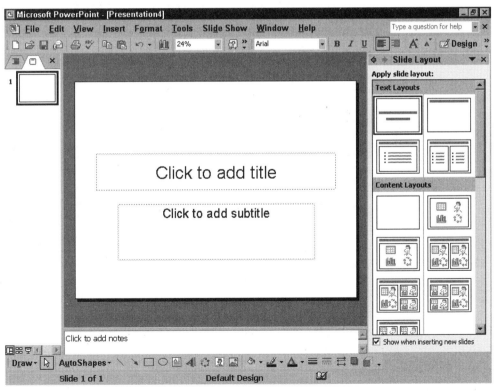

Figure 2-9   Normal view when you create a presentation based only on a blank presentation.

Filling in the outline detail

After you've created the blank presentation file to hold your outline, you are ready to begin building your outline. As noted earlier in this step and in "Step 1: Learn the Logic," an outline is essentially a list of slides you want in your presentation. The outline also includes bullet points for each slide, if appropriate.

To create an outline, follow these steps:

1. Name your presentation.

To create the first title slide of your presentation, click the outline tab in the Outline pane and then click the first slide listed in the Outline pane. This slide shows only a number 1 and a small slide icon. After you select the slide, type the text you want to title or label the first slide of your presentation. Figure 2-10 shows the way Normal view looks after you complete this step.

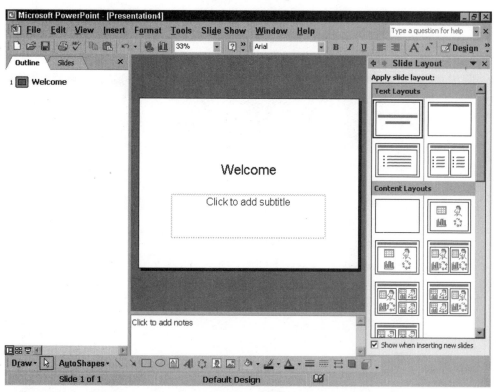

Figure 2-10 Normal view after you add the title slide information to the outline.

NOTE   *PowerPoint uses the title of your first slide to fill the title placeholder on the slide shown in the Slide pane in Normal view.*

2. **Describe the next slide.**

To describe the next slide in your presentation, press the Enter key . PowerPoint adds a new, blank slide to the outline. To give this slide a title, select the slide by clicking; then type the slide title.

You need to describe each of the other slides you want in your presentation. To do this, you can just repeat the process described in the preceding paragraph.

You don't have to add slides to the outline by entering slide titles into the Outline pane. You can also insert a slide by choosing a slide layout from the Slide Layout task pane. To add a slide to your presentation, choose the slide layout that includes the correct set of object placeholders. You can use the Slide Layout task pane to add slides to the outline when you know what object placeholders you want on the slide. You don't *need* to do this, but you can.

3. **Add bulleted lists to slides, as appropriate.**

Presumably, many of your slides will show bulleted text. This bulleted text should also be added to your outline. To add bulleted text to a slide, click the outline tab in the Outline pane and then select the slide by clicking its icon. Then press the End key to move the selection cursor to the end of the slide title. Next, press the Enter key. PowerPoint adds a new line to the outline for the new slide that it assumes you want to add. However, you don't want to add a new slide. You want to add bulleted text to the slide listed on the preceding line of the outline. So press the Tab key. PowerPoint indents the line selected in the outline. Now type the first line of bulleted text. After you've typed the first line, press Enter. PowerPoint inserts a line—only this time it knows that the line is another line of bulleted text. Type this next line of bulleted text. If you need to add additional lines of bulleted text, press Enter again and type again.

To add bulleted text to other slides in your presentation, you follow the same process described in the preceding paragraph. First, you select the slide, and then you create bulleted text by adding lines to the outline—only at a lower, indented level.

Figure 2-11 shows the way this bulleted text looks in the Outline pane. As you would expect, PowerPoint also adds the bulleted text to the slide shown in the Slide pane.

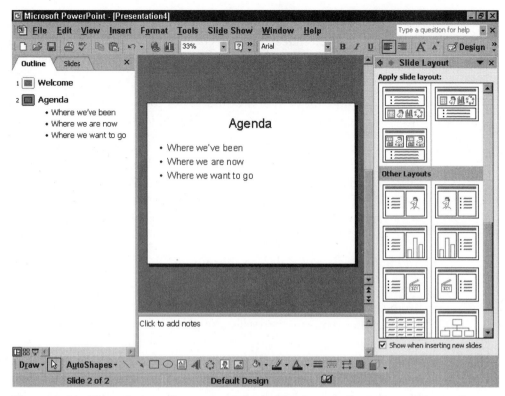

Figure 2-11 Normal view after you add the bulleted text information to the outline.

TIP   *Keep an eye on the slide shown in the Slide pane. You don't have that much space for text on your slides. Practically speaking, you often don't have room for more than a short, punchy title and three or four short bulleted text chunks.*

NOTE   *Later in this step, the section "Working on Your Outline" explains the mechanics of entering text into the outline and then editing the text. Therefore, don't worry too much at this point about doing more than just listing your slides and collecting your most important bulleted text. How you enter and edit text in Outline view is described in detail later.*

TIP *Because people do not read well off walls or screens, keep the number of words in your outline, and therefore on your slides, to an absolute minimum. If everything you are going to say is already on your slides, one of you is unnecessary. Visuals are meant to aid us, not replace us. Therefore, limit the wording on slides to single words or brief phrases and elaborate verbally on what you've written. Complete sentences should be reserved for direct quotations of what someone said or for quoting a law, policy, or legal document. Have the courage to be brief, to omit, and simplify. "Intelligence begins," wrote Marshall McLuhan, "with the ability to condense."*

Reviewing Simple Presentation Strategies

The AutoContent Wizard described earlier is an easy-to-use tool for creating lengthy outlines and structuring large presentations—especially as you start using PowerPoint. You can often employ a simpler strategy, however, when you want to use a presentation to explain, persuade, or recommend. The paragraphs that follow describe simple three-, four-, and five-slide presentations you can create for just these purposes.

Explaining with a Presentation

Speakers find themselves constantly explaining things: a term, a product, a procedure, a service, a policy, a regulation, or anything new. This is one of the most common types of presentation, or part of a presentation, and it lends itself perfectly to PowerPoint slides. Ancient speaking wisdom tells us: "In all things, seek to be clear." To explain anything clearly, answer these questions on your slides.

Slide 1: What?

What are you talking about? Tell them what…

- it is (give a dictionary definition or vivid description)

- it isn't (what it's not; limits; qualifications)

- it's like (compare it to something they already know, or use similes [chattering like a canary]or analogies)

Slide 2: How?

Tell them how...

- it works (how it's made, runs; processes, procedures)

- it's organized (structure, order, arrangement, organization chart)

- it happened (circumstances, the sequence of events)

Slide 3: Why?

Tell them why. What are the reasons this exists? If you are announcing or explaining something new, explain the past: the causes, problems, circumstances, or past events that have led up to the creation of what's new. Explain what the new thing is by answering the What? and How? questions above. Explain the future: the purpose of what's new, the expected outcomes, values, or benefits we hope to gain.

Persuading with a Presentation

We constantly seek to persuade others: to listen to us, to believe what we say, to take the actions we recommend. Here is an original format for persuading that lends itself perfectly to PowerPoint slides. You know the British proverb: You can lead a horse to water, but you can't make him drink. Don't try to make the horse drink, try to make him thirsty. Here's how to create hunger and thirst for your ideas, products, and services.

Slide 1: So that...

First, list the rewards, benefits, gains, protections, or good feelings the person will get by doing what you suggest. Or, name (warn about) the negative consequences the person will avoid by doing as you say. The secret is to begin with benefits, follow with advice, requests, or features. Promise what they'll gain before you tell them what to do.

Slide 2: Do this...

List the specific action, behavior, or performance you want the person or group to take. This should be an action that could be recorded with a video camera—a concrete, observable action—rather than something in the person's mind (like "change your attitude," which can't be verified without visible actions or words).

Slide 3: Instead of...

To clarify your request for action, let the person know what not to do, the exception. Sometimes it's better to express the "instead of" before the "do this." For example, "Instead of trying to create more new customers, why not try to sell more products to existing customers?"

Slide 4: Because...

Finish with the reasons why: the logical, rational, factual, legal, or legitimate reasons why the person should take the action you suggest. This may also be the proof that the benefits you promise are attainable. Sometimes the reason why is because of a law, regulation, or policy. "Because" appeals to our minds, "so that" appeals to our hearts. For example, if you want to maintain the good will of a person who has complained, instead of just apologizing, why not try to make it up to the person by offering something of value. A gift or good-faith offering (reason) may ease the pain of inconvenience the person has suffered, and wins back her trust.

Recommending with a Presentation

When you have a hot new idea or solution you want to recommend and you need a great format for presenting it, try this powerful model that works perfectly with a minimum of five PowerPoint slides.

Slide 1: Burning issue

What's the burning issue? What's the problem you face or the issue at hand? In order to get a handle on any problem, give it to your listeners as a question. For example, if we're discussing finding qualified employees, state this issue as a question. On your *first slide* write: "How can we find more employees who are qualified?" Often the best way to start the question is with the words, "How can we...?" or "What would it take...?"

Slide 2: Background

To help listeners understand the situation, on your second slide describe as much of the background as the audience would need to know to understand the nature and extent of the problem. You might list the known facts. Or answer questions such as, "How long has this been going on? What conclusions can you draw from the facts? What are the consequences of these facts? If we do nothing, what will happen?"

Slide 3: Big idea

What do you recommend? What do you propose to resolve the problem or change the situation? On slide three, state the big idea you've come up with: a suggestion, a new approach, a set of action steps, things to avoid or stop doing, or a next step to take to find out more. This can appear as a statement or a list, with illustrations of your idea or graphic symbols.

Slide 4: Benefits

What benefits can we expect from your big idea? What's the payoff? On slide four list the gains, rewards, positive results, problems solved, advantages, improvements, protections, or satisfactions we can anticipate. Will the benefits you promise offset the possible costs (time, money, efforts, risks)? Slides could also be prepared to show the costs versus benefits of your big idea or advantages/disadvantages. When or how soon can we expect these benefits?

Slide 5: Best thing to do

What's the best thing for the group and its members to do to begin implementing your suggestion? What do you need from them? What would you want them to do to get things going? On slide five, list the specific first steps group members can take. Or, use this step to launch into creative thinking or brainstorming; ask the group, "What would it take for us to bring about this solution? What are all the things we might do?"

NOTE   *These basic steps are an adaptation of ideas developed originally by Ron Hoff in his fine book,* Say It In Six *(1996). Hoff designed them for a presentation lasting six minutes or less. The format could be used for a 30-minute presentation, or in conjunction with a several hour meeting if brainstorming is used. The format has also been tested in college classes and all five steps have been clearly presented in 43 seconds! This also makes a fine structure for a written proposal.*

Importing an Outline

In many cases, PowerPoint can use an outline you've created in another program—such as an outline you've created using your word processing program. If PowerPoint can interpret your outline—because you've used tabs to indicate outline levels or Microsoft Word styles—simply by opening the outline file for PowerPoint, PowerPoint will use the outline as the basis for creating an outline.

NOTE   *When you import an outline, you are in effect starting with a blank presentation and then copying the outline text from the document that contains the outline. Although this method might seem to be a good way to create an outline, especially when you know another program well, it is probably not the best way to work. It's to your advantage to work within PowerPoint to create your presentation outlines because PowerPoint lets you see immediately how much slide text you are adding by using the Slide pane.*

To import an outline, follow these steps:

1. Tell PowerPoint that you want to open the outline document.

To tell PowerPoint that you want to open another document, choose the File menu's Open command. PowerPoint displays the Open dialog box, as shown in Figure 2-12. To tell PowerPoint that you want to look at other types of files (which will include those created by your outlining program), open the Files Of Type list box and select the All Outlines entry.

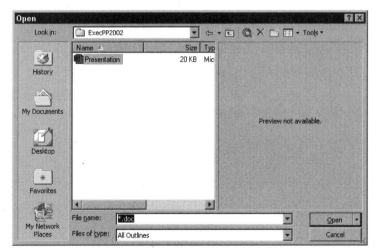

Figure 2-12 The Open dialog box.

2. Locate the folder with the outline document.

After you've done this step, locate the folder that stores the outline document. You can do this by first opening the Look In drop-down list box and then selecting the disk and folder location. If your outline document is stored in a subfolder, you might need to select the subfolder from the list box that appears in the area beneath the Look In drop-down list box.

NOTE   *You can also use the Up One Level button, which appears on the toolbar close to the Look In drop-down list box. The Up One Level button moves you up to the next-higher folder. Or, if you are already at the highest-level folder on a disk, the Up One Level button moves you up to the disk.*

3. Open the outline document.

After you've located the outline document, select it by clicking it and then click the Open button. PowerPoint will import the outline document into PowerPoint and then use its information to build a PowerPoint outline.

NOTE   *In order for PowerPoint to import an outline document, it uses a converter tool. If PowerPoint doesn't have the right converter tool already installed and available for use, you might need to install the converter tool first. To do this, all you need to do is find the Microsoft Office 2002 or Microsoft PowerPoint 2002 CD and insert it into your CD drive. PowerPoint will install the needed converter tool automatically, simply as part of the outline import process.*

After you've imported the outline document, you can work with it in the exact same way as you work with an outline you've created using the AutoContent Wizard or an outline you've created by typing text into the Outline pane. Typically, however, you'll have more work to do with your outline. The next section, "Working on Your Outline," describes how you work with the outline text.

Working on Your Outline

If you used another Windows program, and especially if you have used and become comfortable with another Microsoft Office program, like Microsoft Word, you'll have little trouble working with outline text. In fact, you might want to simply skip this discussion and move ahead to "Step 3: Add Objects." However, if you are not all that comfortable working with the Windows programs or other Microsoft Office programs, you might want to quickly review the following paragraphs. They describe how text editing and outline manipulation works in PowerPoint.

Entering and editing text

You enter and edit text in the Outline pane in the same way as you enter text in other programs. To begin entering text, you first click at the point where you want to enter the text. Windows moves the insertion point to the exact location where you type. Anything you then type gets entered at the insertion point.

By default, PowerPoint inserts text as you type. You can, however, overtype text. To do this, press the Insert key. The Insert key is a toggle switch. By pressing Insert, you toggle between text-insertion mode and text-overtype mode.

If you want to edit text, you generally select the text you want to edit by clicking and dragging. Then you replace the selected text by typing the correct text.

You have a variety of ways to select text. You can click at the first character you want to select and then drag the mouse to the last character you want to select. If you want to select an individual word, you can double-click the word. If you want to select an entire line, you can click the area in front of the line, just in front of the bullet or the slide icon. But note that if you select a slide title line of text, you'll also select the bulleted text.

To delete text, select the text and then choose the Edit menu's Clear command. Or, select the text and then press the Delete key.

Moving and copying text

You can move text by dragging, or you can move text by cutting and pasting. To move text by dragging, first select the text and then point to the text. While you are holding down the mouse button, drag the selected text to its new location.

If you want to copy the text rather than move it, simply hold down the Ctrl key while you drag the text to its new (duplicate) location or use copy and paste.

Moving and copying text by dragging takes some getting used to at first—especially if you are sitting in an airplane and doing it on a laptop computer. But it is actually a pretty handy method after you become comfortable with it.

If you want to copy and move text with menu commands instead, you can use the Edit menu's Copy, Cut, and Paste commands. To move text by using the moving commands, first select text and then choose the Edit menu's Copy command (if you want to copy the text) or Cut command (if you want to move the text). Then position the insertion point at the exact location where you want to move or copy the text and choose the Edit menu's Paste command.

The standard toolbar that PowerPoint supplies provides Copy, Cut, and Paste buttons. You can use these buttons in place of the Edit menu's Copy, Cut, and Paste commands.

NOTE   *If you are not sure which toolbar buttons are which, point to the buttons along the standard toolbar. Any Microsoft Office application displays a pop-up ToolTip box that names the button you are pointing to.*

One confusing feature of Microsoft Office programs is that menu commands and toolbar buttons don't always appear. Microsoft Office programs customize the toolbar and the menu based on commands you are likely to use or have used in the past. Note, however, that if you keep a menu open, Office programs like PowerPoint typically add all the hidden commands.

NOTE   *If you don't want PowerPoint to hide infrequently used menus, choose the Tools menu's Customize command. When PowerPoint displays the Customize dialog box, click the Options tab. Then mark the Show Standard And Formatting Toolbars On Two Rows, and mark the Always Show Full Menus box.*

Using the Outlining toolbar

If you are going to do much work with a PowerPoint outline, use the Outlining toolbar. It provides several useful buttons you can click to make outlining easier. To display the Outlining toolbar, choose the View menu's Toolbar command. PowerPoint displays the Toolbar submenu. To tell PowerPoint that you want to use the Outlining toolbar, choose the Outlining command from the Toolbar submenu. When you do, PowerPoint places a check mark in front of the Outlining command.

Figure 2-13 shows how the PowerPoint program window looks after the Outlining toolbar is added. The Outlining toolbar appears along the left edge of the Outline pane.

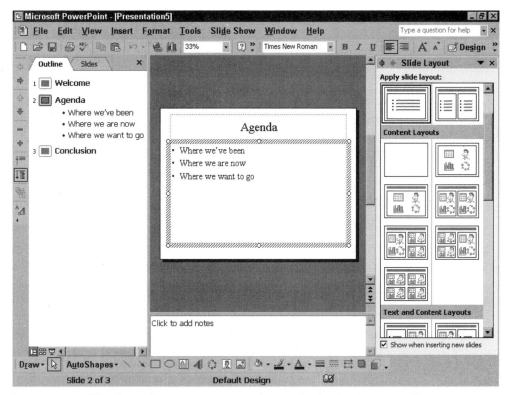

Figure 2-13 The PowerPoint program window with the Outlining toolbar.

NOTE   *If you point to an Outlining toolbar button, PowerPoint displays the button name in a pop-up toolkit box. Use this trick if you are not sure which button is which.*

Promoting and demoting outline levels

The Outlining toolbar provides Promote and Demote buttons—the first two buttons on the Outlining toolbar—for promoting or demoting outline text. To promote outline text, simply select the text you want to promote and click the Promote button. (The Promote button is the arrow that points to the left.) If you promote bulleted text, it moves up to the next-higher level—probably to the level of a slide.

To demote text, predictably, select the text you want to demote and click the Demote button. (The Demote button shows an arrow pointing to the right.) If you demote a slide title, the slide title becomes bulleted text on the preceding slide.

PowerPoint allows you to have bulleted text within a bulleted text list. In other words, you can have bulleted text under a bulleted text item. However, although this situation is technically feasible, practically speaking, slides rarely provide enough information for this level of detail. Typically, the sort of information you might want to place as bulleted text under another bulleted text line should really be spoken information that you provide as you are discussing or talking about the slide.

Moving outline text

The Move Up and Move Down Outlining toolbar buttons let you move text up and down. To move a line of text up, first select the text and then click the Move Up button. The Move Up button is an arrow pointing upward.

If you want to move text down, first select the text and then click the Move Down button. The Move Down button shows an arrow pointing downward.

If you move bulleted text up or down, you simply rearrange the bullet points. However, if you move slides up and down, you rearrange the order of the slides in the presentation.

Collapsing and expanding the outline

The Outlining toolbar provides Collapse and Expand buttons you can use to show more outlining detail and to hide outlining detail. To hide the lower levels of an outline—those levels below the slide title level—select the portion of the outline you want to hide. Then click the Collapse button. The Collapse button shows a minus sign.

If you later want to expand the previously collapsed portion of the outline, select the previously collapsed lines of the outline. Then click the Expand button. The Expand button shows a plus symbol.

Beneath the Collapse and Expand buttons on the Outlining toolbar, PowerPoint provides Collapse All and Expand All buttons. If you click the Collapse All button, PowerPoint collapses the entire outline so that only the slide titles show. If you collapse the entire outline using the Collapse All toolbar button, you can click the Expand All button to later uncollapse the outline.

Summarizing an outline

The second-to-last Outlining toolbar button is the Summary Slide button. If you click the Summary Slide button, PowerPoint adds a summary slide to your outline. If you are going to use this toolbar button, first position the insertion point at the end of your outline, and then click the Summary Slide button. You want the summary slide added to the end of your presentation, and PowerPoint inserts the summary slide, predictably, at the insertion point location.

Showing formatting

The last button on the Outlining toolbar is the Show Formatting tool. If you click the Show Formatting toolbar button, PowerPoint shows the text using the text formatting that PowerPoint is using on the slides. The Show Formatting toolbar button is a toggle switch, so if you click it again, PowerPoint doesn't show the text formatting that will be used on your slides.

Spell-checking your outline

After you finalize your outline, check the spelling. Remember that your outline text appears on your slides, and there is no easier time to check your spelling than when you complete the outline.

To check your spelling, use the Tools menu's Spelling command. If PowerPoint discovers no misspellings, it displays a dialog box telling you simply that the spelling check is complete (see Figure 2-14). That is what you want to see.

Figure 2-14 The Spelling Check Is Complete message box.

If PowerPoint finds one or more spelling errors, it displays the Spelling dialog box, as shown in Figure 2-15. PowerPoint will use the Not In Dictionary text box to identify the word that appears to be misspelled. PowerPoint selects this word in the outline. To fix the spelling, you can type the correct spelling in the Change To box. Or, you can select one of the words listed in the Suggestions list box. PowerPoint fills the Change To box initially with its best guess about the correct spelling.

Figure 2-15 The Spelling dialog box.

After you or PowerPoint have entered the correct spelling in the Change To box, click the Change button to correct the misspelling. Or, if you want to change the spelling everywhere it appears in the outline, click the Change All button.

If the word is not really a misspelling, you can click the Ignore button to ignore the single occurrence that was found or the Ignore All button to ignore every occurrence in the outline.

If you are using words that are correctly spelled but are not in the spelling dictionary—this might be the case if you are clicking the Ignore or the Ignore All buttons—you can click the Add button. When you click the Add button, PowerPoint adds the word shown in the Not In Dictionary box to its custom spelling dictionary. You typically add things like people's names and specialized business or industry terms to the custom spelling dictionary.

If the Spelling command identifies a misspelling but doesn't identify the correct spelling using its Suggestions box, you can try to get additional suggestions. To do this, enter another guess at the spelling into the Change To box, and then click the Suggest button. PowerPoint will use the word you entered into the Change To box to look for other suggested spellings.

Saving and Later Opening Your Outline

After you create your outline, make editorial changes, and then check its accuracy and spelling, you will of course want to save the outline and the presentation it's part of. To do this, simply choose the File menu's Save command. PowerPoint displays the Save As dialog box, as shown in Figure 2-16.

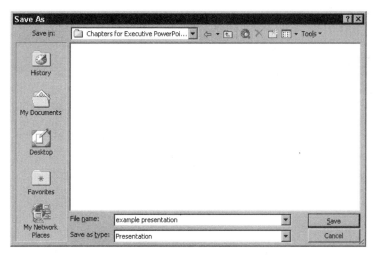

Figure 2-16 The Save As dialog box.

To save your presentation, click the Save In drop-down list box to choose a folder location for the presentation. Then use the File Name box to give your presentation a name. After you've identified the appropriate folder location and named the presentation, click the Save button. PowerPoint saves your presentation in the specified location using the name you have provided.

To later open your outline, you choose the File menu's Open command. When PowerPoint displays the Open dialog box, use its Look In drop-down list box to identify the folder location of the presentation. Then double-click the presentation on the list beneath the Look In drop-down list box. Figure 2-17 shows the Open dialog box.

Figure 2-17 The Open dialog box.

Step 3

ADD OBJECTS

Featuring:

- Using Tables
- Using Pictures
- Using Charts
- Using Organization Charts
- Using Other Objects on Slides

After you outline your content, as described in "Step 2: Outline Your Content," you typically add objects to your slides. *Objects* are simply tables, pictures, charts, and other graphical elements you'll use to communicate or help communicate your message.

Using Tables

A *table* is a grid of columns and rows. The cells that make up the table—a *cell* is the intersection of a column and row—can contain text, number values, or even pictures. Tables are powerful tools for organizing information, and, in fact, people and businesses commonly use tables to display information—especially quantitative information, like financial data.

Adding a table

To add a table to a slide, follow these steps:

1. Select the slide.

Assuming that you've displayed the presentation using Normal view, you can select the slide in several different ways. One way is to click the slide in the Outline pane. If you do this, PowerPoint displays the slide in the Slide pane. PowerPoint also selects the slide title in the Outline pane. You can also select a slide by clicking the scroll bar along the right edge of the Slide pane. As you do this, PowerPoint pages through the slides of your presentation. Click above the scroll marker to page up. Click below the scroll bar marker to page down.

NOTE   *You can also drag the scroll bar marker to move back and forth through the slides of your presentation and click the arrow buttons at either end of the scroll bar to move forward and backward a slide at a time.*

2. Tell PowerPoint that you want to insert a table.

After you select a slide to which you want to add a table, choose the Insert menu's Table command. PowerPoint displays the Insert Table dialog box, as shown in Figure 3-1.

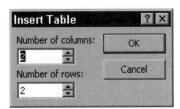

Figure 3-1   The Insert Table dialog box.

3. Describe the table size.

Table size is determined by two simple quantities: the number of columns in the table and the number of rows in the table. Use the Number Of Columns box to tell PowerPoint how many columns the new table needs. Use the Number Of Rows box to tell PowerPoint how many rows the new table needs. After you specify these dimensions, click OK. PowerPoint then adds the table to the open slide (see Figure 3-2).

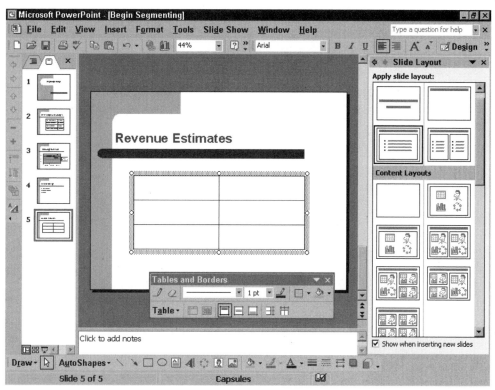

Figure 3-2 The empty table.

4. Fill the table with information.

After PowerPoint adds the table to the slide, you can fill the slide table with information. To do this, click a table cell. Then enter into the cell the information you want. To fill another cell with information, click it and then enter information there. Figure 3-3 shows a filled table.

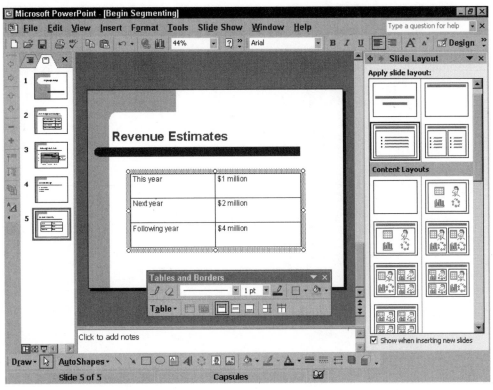

Figure 3-3   The filled table.

NOTE   *You can also use the Edit menu's Cut, Copy, and Paste commands, as well as the toolbar's Cut, Copy, and Paste buttons to move text and even pictures or clipart into the cells of a table you just inserted. To use the Cut, Copy, and Paste commands, first select whatever it is you want to cut or copy and choose the Cut or Copy command. Next, click the cell into which you want to paste the text or item you've just cut or copied. Finally, choose the Edit menu's Paste command or click the Paste toolbar button.*

Positioning and sizing a table

After the table holds its information, you can to resize it and then reposition it so that it looks right and looks like it is in place.

To resize the table, take the following steps:

1. Select the table.

To verify that the table is selected, click it. When PowerPoint selects the table, it adds a thick border to the outside edge of the table. Figure 3-4 shows this type of table selected.

This year	$1 million
Next year	$2 million
Following year	$4 million

Figure 3-4   A table with selection handles.

2. Resize the table.

After you've selected a table, you can resize it by dragging the selection handles that appear at the corners of the table and at the midpoints of each of the sides of the table. If you have questions, experiment with a table in a sample PowerPoint slide to see how this process works. Essentially, all you do is drag a selection handle up or down, back and forth, or in and out. As you drag a selection handle, PowerPoint resizes the table.

3. Resize the table's columns and rows.

After you've sized the table so that the overall height and width dimensions are correct, resize the columns and rows of the table's interior by clicking and dragging the interior row and column borders. When you point to an interior column border or row border, PowerPoint changes the mouse pointer icon. After PowerPoint changes the icon to a double-headed arrow, click the mouse button and drag the interior column border or row border the way you want to resize it.

To move a table, follow these steps:

1. Select the table.

To verify that the table is selected, click it. PowerPoint selects the table, adding a thick border to the outside edge of the table, as shown in Figure 3-4.

2. Move the table.

To move the table, point to the outside border of the table—the border that shows the thick selection border—and then drag the table to the correct location. After the table is in the correct position, simply release the mouse button.

TIP   *When you add an object like a table, clipart, photo, or image to a slide, you might wonder, "Where should I put it?" Because we read from top to bottom and from left to right, place the image either at the* top *or to the* left *(or* top left*). An old advertising design formula commonly places the picture at the top, the headline underneath the picture, and the text (or copy) below the picture. Experiment. But you'll never go wrong beginning with the picture in the top left position and the text in the bottom right position and moving things around until the design seems right.*

Formatting a table

When you insert a table into a slide, PowerPoint adds or opens the Tables And Borders toolbar, as shown in Figure 3-5. You can use this toolbar's buttons and boxes to change the format of the table. In fact, the steps that follow simply describe this toolbar's tools from left to right.

NOTE   *You can point to any tool to display the tool's name in a pop-up ToolTip box.*

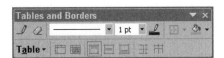

Figure 3-5   The Tables And Borders toolbar.

To format a table using the Table And Borders toolbar, take the following steps:

1. **Add any rows or columns that are needed.**

   To add a column or row to an existing table, click the Draw Table tool, which shows a pencil drawing a line on the face of the Tool button. Then draw a line where the new border should be created.

   If you draw a line that cuts off text in a table cell, PowerPoint might split your text, putting one part of the text in one cell and the other, cut-off part of the text in another cell.

2. **Erase any cell borders that aren't needed.**

   To erase a line in a table that separates two cells, click the Eraser toolbar button. PowerPoint changes the mouse pointer to an eraser icon. Use the eraser icon to erase the table border you don't want in the table.

3. Specify how the table borders should look.

The Tables And Borders toolbar provides three tools for controlling the way the table borders look: the Border Style list box, the Border Width list box, and the Border Color button.

To change the way the table borders look, open the Border Style list box and choose the border style you want.

To change the weight or width of the table borders, open the Border Width list box and choose a border width specification.

To change the color of the table borders, click the Border Color button. When PowerPoint displays a pop-up box of colored squares, click the square that is the color you want for the table's borders.

After you've used these three toolbar tools to specify the style, thickness, and color of your table's borders, you click the Draw Table button. Then you use the Draw Table tool to trace over the border you want to format according to the current Border Style, Border Width, and Border Color specifications.

4. Specify how the outside border should look.

The Tables And Borders toolbar provides an Outside Borders tool you can use to select where you want borders drawn. To use this tool, click the down-arrow button that appears to the right of the toolbar button. When PowerPoint displays a box showing pictures of the various table borders in a table, click the picture that most closely shows the table borders you want to change to match the current Border Style, Border Width, and Border Color settings.

5. Change the table's fill color.

To change the color used to fill in the interior of a table, you use the Fill Color tool. If you just want to accept PowerPoint's suggested fill color, you can click the Fill Color button. If you want to choose a fill color, you need to click the small button just to the right of the Fill Color tool. When you click this button, PowerPoint displays the box that shows colored squares. The colored squares identify the color you want to use for the cells in the table.

NOTE   *Click the Table button on the Tables And Borders toolbar to display a menu of commands you can use to insert and delete table rows and columns.*

6. As needed, merge and split table cells.

You can combine the selected cells in a table by clicking the Merge Cells tool. You can split the selected table cell into two cells by clicking the Split Cell tool.

7. **Specify how text should be aligned in the table.**

The text you enter into table cells can be aligned in various ways. To align table text, first select the text or the row or column with the text. You can do this step by clicking and dragging the mouse. After you select the text, you specify what alignment should be used. If you want to align text against the top edge of the table cells, click the Align Top button. If you want to align text in the center of the cell, click the Center Vertically toolbar button. If you want the text to align or abut against the bottom of a cell, click the Align Bottom button.

8. **As needed, evenly distribute table rows and columns.**

To create evenly spaced, or distributed, table rows, click the Distribute Rows Evenly tool. To create evenly spaced, or distributed, table columns, click the Distribute Columns Evenly tool.

Using Pictures

You can add pictures to slides. These pictures can come from either the Clip Art Gallery that comes with PowerPoint or the images you've collected and stored on your computer or network.

Adding clip art

Microsoft Office and PowerPoint come with a rich library of clip art. This library includes photographs, line drawings, and even video.

To add a clip art object to your slide, take these steps:

1. **Tell PowerPoint you want to add clip art.**

Choose the Insert menu's Picture command and then the Clip Art command from the Picture submenu. When you choose this ClipArt command, PowerPoint displays the Insert Clip Art task pane, as shown in Figure 3-6.

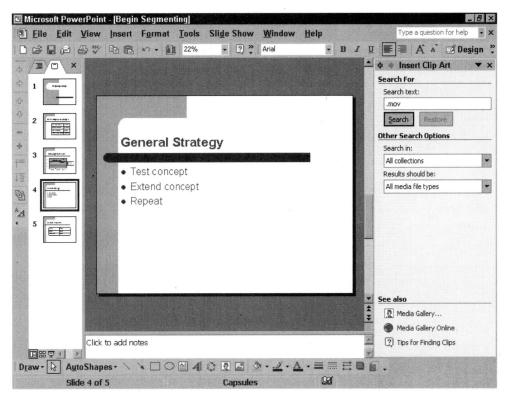

Figure 3-6   The Insert Clip Art task pane.

2. Build a list of clip art images.

Use the Search Text box, the Search In drop-down list box, and the Results Should Be drop-down list box to describe the sorts of clip art pictures you're looking for. You can enter the word "building" in the Search Text box, for example, to tell PowerPoint you want to see pictures of buildings. Then click the Search button. PowerPoint builds a list of clip art pictures matching your search criteria. Figure 3-7, for example, shows a portion of the "building" clip art images that PowerPoint supplies.

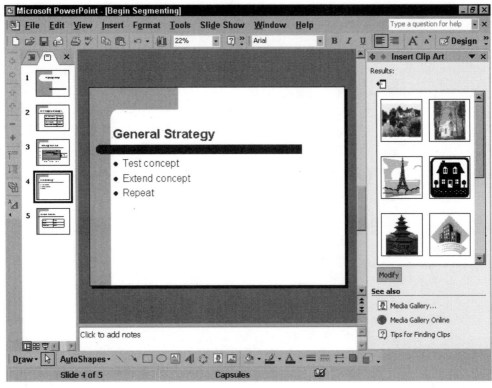

Figure 3-7   The Insert Clip Art task pane showing buildings clips.

3. Select the image.

You can scroll through the images displayed in the Insert Clip Art task pane to find the one you want to use.

To add the image you select to your slide, right-click the image to display the Short-cuts menu, and then choose the Insert command from the Shortcuts menu. PowerPoint adds the clip art image to your slide.

If you want to add another image, repeat steps 2 and 3.

4. Move the image to its correct location.

You can move a clip art image by dragging it. You can resize a clip art image by first selecting it and then dragging the selection handles as shown in Figure 3-8. Moving and resizing a clip art image isn't difficult. If you have questions, simply experiment by pointing, clicking, and dragging the mouse pointer.

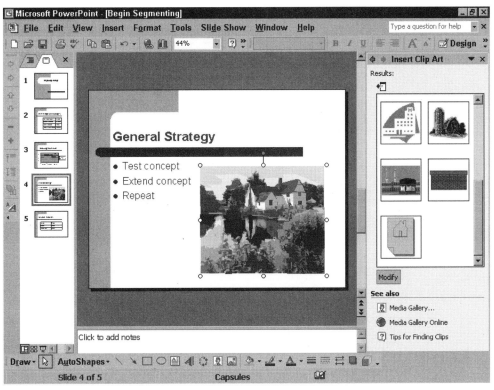

Figure 3-8   A slide with a clip art picture

Adding pictures

You can add pictures, such as photographic images, to a PowerPoint slide. The only prerequisite is that the picture file must be stored somewhere on your hard disk.

To insert a picture onto a slide, take these steps:

1. Tell PowerPoint that you want to add a picture.

Choose the Insert menu's Picture command. Then, when PowerPoint displays the Picture submenu, choose its From File command. PowerPoint displays the Insert Picture dialog box, as shown in Figure 3-9.

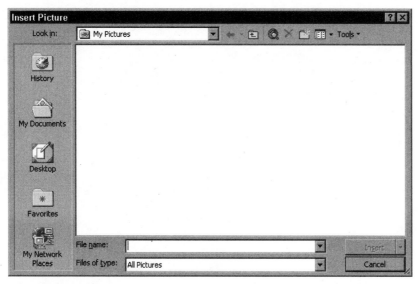

Figure 3-9   The Insert Picture dialog box.

2. Identify the location of the picture.

Use the Look In box to identify the folder location of the picture.

3. Insert the picture.

After you identify the correct folder location, you'll see the image listed in the list box beneath the Look In box. You can insert the image by clicking its filename and then clicking the Insert button. Or you can double-click the filename.

4. Move the image to its correct location.

As is the case with clip art images, you can move the inserted picture by dragging it. You can also resize the inserted picture by first clicking it and then dragging the selection handles that PowerPoint adds to the corners and sides of the image.

Changing clip art images and pictures

After you insert a clip art image or picture onto a slide, PowerPoint adds the Picture toolbar to the PowerPoint program window (see Figure 3-10).

Figure 3-10   The Picture toolbar.

The Picture toolbar provides tools you can use to change the selected clip art image or picture, as described in this list:

- The Insert Picture From File button lets you insert a second picture. This button is equivalent to the From File command on the Picture submenu.

- The Image Control Picture toolbar button displays a list of image-editing options from which you can choose. Just experiment to see what effect they have.

- The More Contrast and Less Contrast toolbar buttons increase the contrast of a picture.

- The More Brightness and Less Brightness buttons darken or lighten a picture image.

- The Crop button might let you crop a portion of an image.

- The Rotate Left button lets you rotate a picture one-quarter turn left.

- The Line Style button displays a menu of lines you can use for an image border.

- The Compress Pictures button lets you reduce the size of pictures by reducing the resolution and by deleting cropped areas of the picture.

- The Recolor Picture button might let you recolor an image—although this won't be possible with all images.

- The Format Picture button displays a dialog box you can use to change elements of the picture, such as its brightness, contrast, and other characteristics.

- The Set Transparent Color tool lets you tell PowerPoint to remove whatever color you want from the image you click. To use the Set Transparent Color tool, click the tool and then click the color you want to make transparent.

- The Reset Picture tool resets the picture to its original condition.

Using Charts

PowerPoint comes with a charting tool named Microsoft Graph. Graph lets you produce charts that you can then use on your PowerPoint slides.

NOTE *Appendix A describes how to use Microsoft Graph in more detail.*

Understanding how Graph sees data

To use Graph, you should first understand three terms: data values, data series, and data categories.

Data values are the simplest components to understand. In Figure 3-11, for example, data values are the numbers, or numeric values, that Microsoft Graph will use to create bars, columns, or lines that visually represent the data.

NOTE   *The datasheet shown in Figure 3-11 is what you'll actually use to collect the to-be-plotted data.*

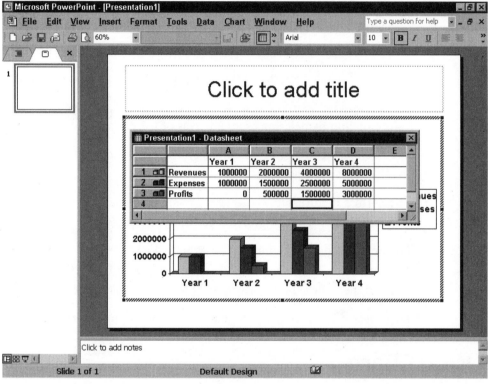

Figure 3-11 The PowerPoint window showing a datasheet with some sample data values.

Data series is the second graphing term you need to understand. Data series, in a nutshell, identify the information you're plotting on a chart. In Figure 3-11, the data series are Revenues (shown in row 1), Expenses (shown in row 2), and Profits (shown in row 3).

If you ask the question "What does my chart show?", every one-word an-swer typically identifies a data series. In the case of the datasheet shown in Figure 3-11, for example, if you asked this question, you would answer correctly by saying that revenues, expenses, and profits are the three data series.

Data categories is the third term you need to understand. Data categories are often a little difficult to understand or to interpret correctly the first time you encounter them. Simply stated, however, data categories organize the data values in the data series. The datasheet shown in Figure 3-11, for example, uses the years 1, 2, 3, and 4 to organize the revenue, expenses, and profits data values. Years are this data's data categories.

Charts don't have to use time periods, such as years, however, to organize the data values in each of the data series. Take a look at the datasheet shown in Figure 3-12. It uses the same data series and, in fact, the same data values, but uses different data category names. In Figure 3-12, the data category names are fictitious company divisions: West, East, North, and South.

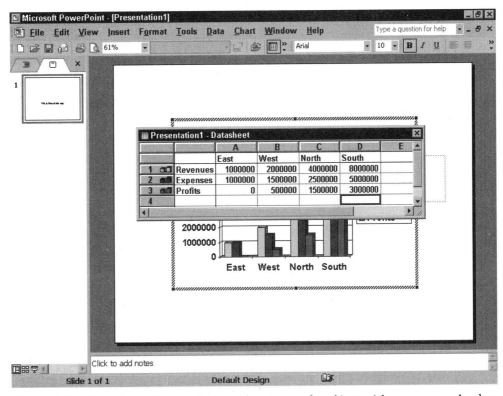

Figure 3-12 The PowerPoint window showing a datasheet with some sample data values and non-time data categories.

NOTE   *In any chart that shows how data values change over time, the data category is time, which means that the data category names will be time period identifiers. You might use year numbers such as 2000, 2001, and 2002, for example. You might also use textual labels, such as year 1, year 2, and year 3. You might chart data over smaller time intervals, such as by day, by week, or by month. A chart, or graph, that uses time as the data category, by the way, is called a* time-series chart, *or* graph.

Adding a chart

To add a chart to a slide, follow these steps:

1. **Select the slide to which you want to add the chart.**

   If you're using Normal view to work with your presentation, you can select the slide to which you want to add the chart by clicking the slide title in the Outline pane. You can also scroll through the individual slides shown in the Slide pane by dragging the Slide pane's scroll bar marker. Or you can click the scroll bar buttons.

2. **Tell PowerPoint that you want to add a chart.**

   Choose the Insert menu's Chart command to tell PowerPoint that you want to add a chart to the displayed slide. When you do this step, PowerPoint displays the Datasheet window and adds a placeholder to the center of the displayed slide. Figure 3-13 shows the way this element looks before you begin making changes.

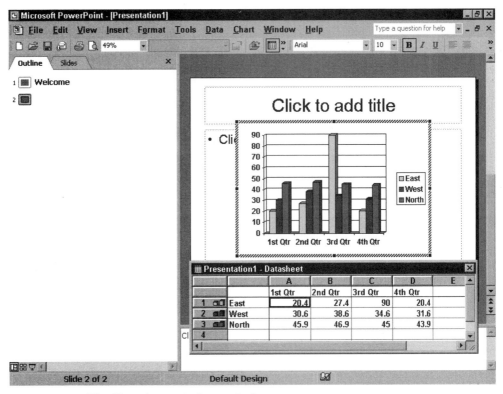

Figure 3-13 The Datasheet window as it first appears.

3. Provide the data you want to plot in a chart.

You use the datasheet to describe the data you want to plot in a chart. The datasheet, which looks like a small spreadsheet, or table, lets you collect the actual data values you will plot, data series names, and data category names.

Use the first column for the data series names. Use the first unnumbered row of the datasheet for the data category names. Use each numbered row for a data series.

After you enter the data values, data series names, and data category names information into the datasheet, you can close the datasheet. Microsoft Graph uses the datasheet information to redraw the graph shown in the placeholder. Figure 3-14 shows how the chart looks on a slide before you begin making changes. (For Figure 3-14, we've closed the Outline pane and the task pane to make more room for the chart.)

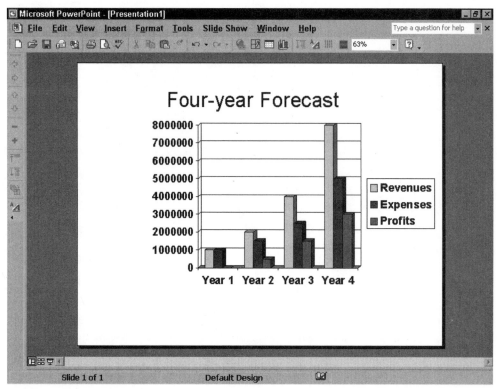

Figure 3-14 A chart object on a slide.

4. Specify the chart type.

Microsoft Graph initially plots your data in a three-dimensional bar chart, but Graph supplies more than a dozen types of charts. To choose or review the available chart types, first verify that the chart object is selected. (If it isn't, click it to select it.) Then choose the Chart menu's Chart Type command. PowerPoint displays the Chart Type dialog box, as shown in Figure 3-15. You use this dialog box to choose the type of chart you want. To make this specification, you first select a chart type from the Chart Type list box. Then you choose a chart subtype by clicking one of the chart subtype pictures to the right of the Chart Type list box. After you've selected a chart type and chart subtype, click the OK button to make your change.

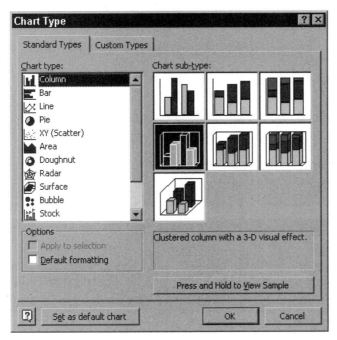

Figure 3-15 The Chart Type dialog box.

NOTE *Appendix A, "Creating Better Charts with Microsoft Graph," provides addi-tional information on choosing an appropriate chart type given the data you are working with and the message you want to convey. If you're new to chart-ing, you might want to read that appendix for some useful ideas.*

Customizing a chart

After you choose the chart type, you can customize the chart so that it best meets your presentation requirements. To do this, click the chart object to select it. Choose the Chart menu's Chart Options command. Microsoft Graph displays the Chart Options dia-log box, as shown in Figure 3-16. The Chart Options dialog box lets you customize the chart in almost any way imaginable. The following paragraphs quickly describe the customizations you have available.

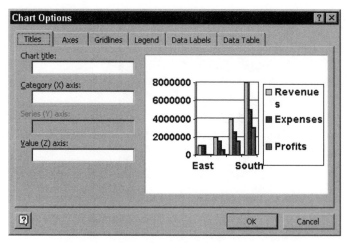

Figure 3-16 The Chart Options dialog box showing the Titles tab.

The Titles tab, which is shown in Figure 3-16, lets you add text to the chart object to label the chart and the chart axis. You often won't do this, but if you want to title the chart, you can enter a title. If you need to label the chart axis to more clearly describe what is being plotted, you can also do this by using the Titles tab.

The Axes tab, as shown in Figure 3-17, provides check boxes and three option buttons you can click or mark or unmark to tell Microsoft Graph whether you want an axis on the chart—and, when you do, how the axis should be drawn. The Axes tab, like the other tabs in the Chart Options dialog box, redraw the picture of the chart using your current specifications. Therefore, your best course of action is often to simply experiment with different axis settings. You can see which work best for your data.

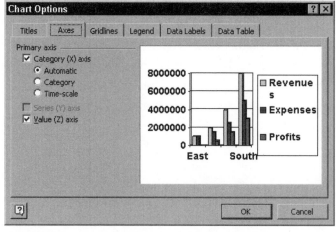

Figure 3-17 The Chart Options dialog box showing the Axes tab.

The Gridlines tab, as shown in Figure 3-18, lets you add horizontal and vertical gridlines to your chart or remove them. To add or remove gridlines, you mark and unmark check boxes. As with other chart options settings, you can conveniently experiment by marking and unmarking check boxes. The Chart Options tab includes a picture of your chart that shows your current chart options settings.

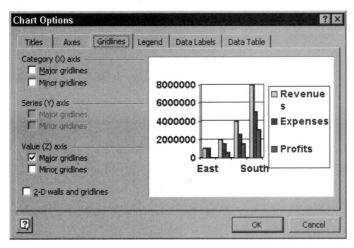

Figure 3-18 The Chart Options dialog box showing the Gridlines tab.

The Legend tab, as shown in Figure 3-19, lets you specify whether you want a legend. If you do, the Legend tab lets you choose a location for the legend. To specify whether you want the legend, you mark the check box. To choose a legend location, you click an option button.

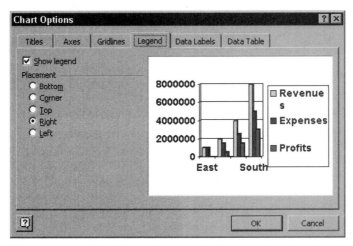

Figure 3-19 The Chart Options dialog box showing the Legend tab.

The Data Labels tab, as shown in Figure 3-20, provides check boxes you can mark to indicate whether data markers should be labeled with the actual values they are supposed to plot. The Data Labels tab also provides a Separator box you can use to specify which symbol Graph uses to separate thousands and a Legend Key box you can use to put a legend next to data markers. The *data marker* is the graphics element a chart uses to visually represent a data value. In a bar chart, for example, the bar is the data marker.

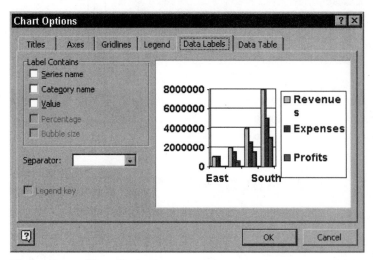

Figure 3-20 The Chart Options dialog box showing the Data Labels tab.

The Data Table tab, as shown in Figure 3-21, lets you add a data table to your chart. For charts you add to PowerPoint slides, data tables would be used infrequently. A data table shows the actual plotted values in a table—not unlike the datasheet from which the plotted data comes. To specify whether you want or don't want a data table, you mark and unmark check boxes.

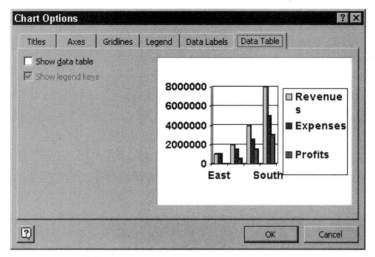

Figure 3-21 The Chart Options dialog box showing the Data Table tab.

Using Organization Charts

PowerPoint also lets you add organization chart objects to slides.

Adding an organization chart

To add an organization chart to a slide, follow these steps:

1. Select the slide.

If you're using Normal view to work with your presentation, you can select the slide you want to add the organization chart to by clicking the slide title in the Outline pane. You can also scroll through the individual slides shown in the Slide pane by dragging the Slide pane's scroll bar marker or by clicking the scroll bar buttons.

2. Tell PowerPoint that you want to add an organization chart.

Choose the Insert menu's Picture command. When PowerPoint displays the Picture submenu, choose its Organization Chart command. PowerPoint adds an organization chart object to the slide and displays the Organization Chart toolbar, as shown in Figure 3-22. (In Figure 3-22, we've closed the Outline pane and the task pane to make more room for the organization chart object.)

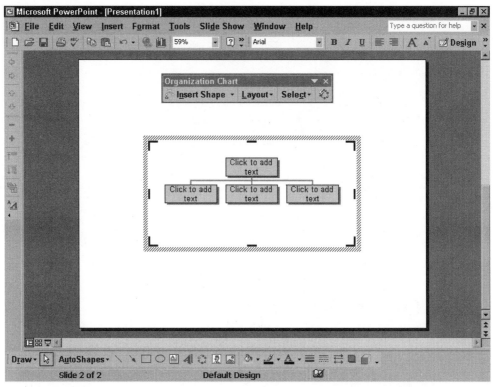

Figure 3-22 The PowerPoint window showing an organization chart object.

3. Describe the organization's structure.

Each of the boxes on the organization chart represents a position. Some positions are manager positions, and some positions are subordinate positions. Although the Organization Chart program initially creates a rough guess of your organizational structure, you need to update this organizational structure to reflect reality. You do this by removing any unneeded boxes and then adding any new, necessary boxes.

- To add a subordinate position, click the box that represents the subordinate's manager. For example, if you want to add a fourth subordinate to the Manager box, you click the Subordinate button and then the Manager box. Then click the Insert Shape tool on the Organization Chart toolbar and choose Subordinate from the menu.

- To add a coworker to a position, click the position that has the coworker. Then click the Insert Shape tool on the Organization Chart toolbar and choose Coworker from the menu.

- The Organization Chart toolbar also supplies an Assistant button. You can use the Assistant button to add an Assistant Position box to some other position box. First click the position with an assistant. Then click the Insert Shape tool and choose Assistant from the menu.

NOTE *The buttons you use to add subordinates, coworkers, and assistants aren't difficult to use, and your best bet is simply to experiment with them. You can remove any organization position box simply by clicking it and then choosing the Edit menu's Cut command or by pressing the Delete key.*

4. Describe individual positions.

After you describe the organizational structure, you need to describe the positions in more detail. To do this, click a position box. When you do, Microsoft Organization Chart turns the box into a text box. Type the position information you want. Typically, you put the name of the person filling the position on the first line and put the person's title on the second line. If you want, you can also include a line or two of comment or general information. You can edit this position box text in the same way you edit text anywhere else. You then need to continue to describe the other positions. Figure 3-23 shows a simple but completed organization chart.

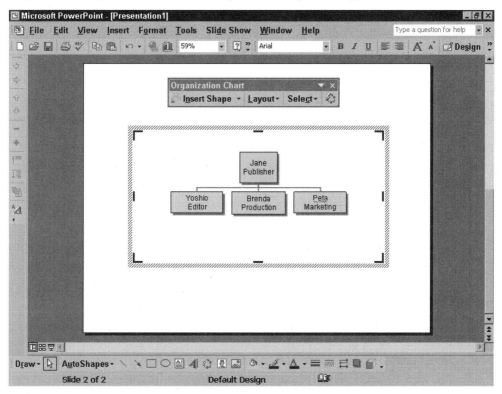

Figure 3-23 A simple organization chart.

Customizing an organization chart

Not surprisingly, Organization Chart objects can be customized in a variety of ways. Most of these customization options are straightforward. Nevertheless, let's quickly describe how you can make some of the most important changes to your organization chart's appearance.

Changing the chart layout

The Layout menu displays a menu of pictures that show the various organization chart styles you can use. This definition is too circular, but choose the Layout menu and take a look at the menu of picture buttons that are displayed for the Standard, Both Hanging, Left Hanging, and Right Hanging commands. What these Layout menu commands do becomes clear. All you need to do is choose a button that shows a picture of what you want your chart to resemble.

The Layout menu also includes four commands for resizing and rearranging the organization chart, its boxes, and its lines: Fit Organization Chart To Contents, Expand Organization Chart, Scale Organization Chart, and AutoLayout. Again, these commands show pictures that explain what they do. You choose the command that shows a picture of what you want.

Formatting organization chart text

To format text in an organization chart object, first select the position box or boxes you want to reformat. You can select one position box by clicking it. If you want to select all position boxes, or some group of them, choose the Select menu command that corresponds to the group of position boxes you want to arrange.

After you've selected the position boxes you want to change, you can use the Format menu's Font command to change the font. When you choose the Format menu's Font command, PowerPoint displays the Font dialog box, as shown in Figure 3-24. You can use its three boxes (Font, Font Style, and Size) to specify how you want text in the selected position box or boxes to appear. Select the font you want to use from the Font list box, the style you want from the Font Style list box, and the point size you want from the Size list box. If you want to add special effects to the text in the selected boxes, mark the Effects boxes: Underline, Shadow, Emboss, and so on.

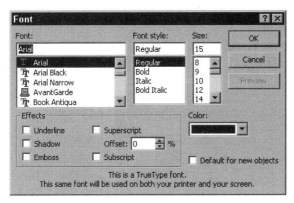

Figure 3-24 The Font dialog box.

NOTE *The Size box and list box refer to point size. A point equals 1/72 inch.*

To change the color of organization chart text, select a color from the Color drop-down list box. Or, if none of the colors listed is what you want, choose the More Colors option from the Colors drop-down list box. PowerPoint displays the Colors dialog box, as shown in Figure 3-25. To use one of the colors shown for the text in the selected box or boxes, click the color.

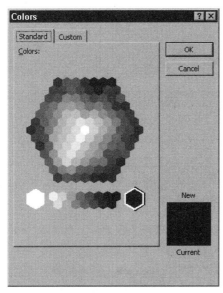

Figure 3-25 The Colors dialog box.

Changing boxes and lines

You can change the appearance of the selected position box or boxes, line or lines by right-clicking the box or line and then choosing the Format AutoShape command from the Shortcuts menu. When PowerPoint displays the Format Auto Shape dialog box, as shown in Figure 3-26, you use its tabs, buttons, and boxes to change characteristics like color and line thickness.

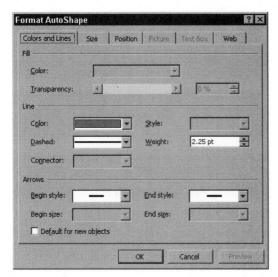

Firure 3-26   The Format AutoShape dialog box.

TIP   *"Step 4: Design Your Look" discusses the Format AutoShape command and dialog box in some detail in its section, "Formatting an Object." Refer there if you have questions.*

Using Other Objects on Slides

In addition to table, picture, chart, and organization chart objects, you can add other types of objects to slides. The objects already discussed in this step are those you will most commonly use, but let's briefly describe some other objects and how to add them.

Using the Insert Object command

If you choose the Insert menu's Object command, PowerPoint displays the Insert Object dialog box, as shown in Figure 3-27. You can use this dialog box to create a new object from scratch using some other program you have installed on your computer. You can also use this dialog box to grab an existing file and use it as an object on a slide.

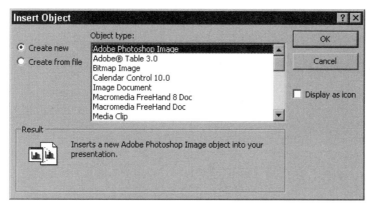

Figure 3-27 The Insert Object dialog box.

To create a brand-new object using a program already on your computer, click the Create New button. Then select the object type from the list box. When you click OK, PowerPoint opens the appropriate program and you use it to create the object you want.

To use an existing file as an object, click the Create From File button. Then use the File box (not shown) to identify the file location and name.

Adding Microsoft Office objects

You can easily use objects created in other Microsoft Office programs, such as chunks of Word documents, ranges from Excel worksheets, and charts from another program like Excel. There are several different ways you can grab one of these other objects and use it in a PowerPoint slide—including the Insert Object command that was just discussed. However, the easiest way to use one of these other objects is by following these steps:

1. Copy the object.

Display the object or the document that provides the object using the native program. For example, if you want to copy an Excel chart, start Excel, open the workbook with the chart, select the chart, and then choose the Edit menu's Copy command. You would use this same rough sequence of steps to copy any other object, too.

2. Paste the object onto the appropriate PowerPoint slide.

After you've copied the object you want to use on a PowerPoint slide, start PowerPoint, open the appropriate PowerPoint presentation, select the slide on which you want to paste the object, and then choose the Edit menu's Paste command.

NOTE *Because the Copy and Paste commands make copying an object from one program to another extremely easy, you'll find it most efficient to create objects for PowerPoint slides using those programs you know best. For example, if you are proficient in using Excel, you probably would want to use Excel to create charts for your PowerPoint presentations. Not only is Excel more capable and powerful in terms of its chart-creation capabilities, but you also already know how to use the program.*

Adding drawn objects

Managers and professionals who use PowerPoint are unlikely to draw objects for slides. Most of us, quite frankly, don't have artistic skills or the time to add this type of embellishment to our presentations. Nevertheless, you should at least know that PowerPoint will let you draw objects and include objects on slides. To do this, you choose the Insert menu's Picture command. Then, when PowerPoint displays the Picture submenu, you choose the AutoShapes command. When you choose this command, PowerPoint displays the AutoShapes toolbar, as shown in Figure 3-28. It provides a bunch of previously drawn shapes and images you can select and then use on a PowerPoint slide.

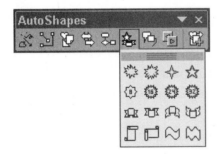

Figure 3-28 The AutoShapes toolbar with the Stars And Banners menu open.

You can also use the Drawing toolbar to draw freehand shapes and images for use on a slide. To display the Drawing toolbar, choose the View menu's Toolbar command. Then choose the Drawing command from the Toolbar's submenu. When you do this, PowerPoint adds the Drawing toolbar to the PowerPoint program window, as shown in Figure 3-29. The Drawing toolbar includes roughly two dozen clickable buttons you can use to draw objects by hand.

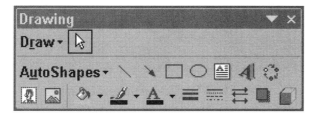

Figure 3-29 The Drawing toolbar.

Adding WordArt objects

You can take a chunk of text and turn it into a WordArt object. When you do this, the text still looks like text but is actually a fancy, often colorful graphics object, as shown in Figure 3-30. Appendix B, "Using WordArt," describes the WordArt applet in more detail.

Figure 3-30 A WordArt object.

Step 4

DESIGN YOUR LOOK

Featuring:

- Selecting a Design Template
- Customizing the Master Slides
- Formatting an Object
- Working with Special Placeholders
- Using the Formatting Toolbar

The earlier discussions in this book focused on developing content for your presentations—which is only appropriate. A good presentation is fundamentally based on good, rich, interesting content. But the look or design of your presentation is important, too, so in this step we turn from the content of your presentation to its design and, specifically, the tools that PowerPoint supplies to make your presentations professional and appropriate in appearance.

NOTE   *Your presentation's slides might already look the way you want. When you created your new presentation using PowerPoint, you might have based your presentation on an existing design template, and that design template might give you just the look you want. If that's the case in your situation, skip ahead to "Step 5: Add Special Effects."*

Selecting a Design Template

PowerPoint supplies design templates. A *design template* provides a color scheme that is used for all the presentation's slides; the *title master slide,* which shows how your title slide looks; and a *slide master slide,* which shows how the nontitle slides in your presentation look.

You can choose a design template in two ways. Which way you choose the design template depends on whether you're just starting to create your presentation or have already created the presentation.

Selecting a design template as you start

One way—and perhaps the most common—is to select a design template before you begin creating your presentation. When you start PowerPoint, it displays the task pane shown in Figure 4-1. This New Presentation task pane lets you indicate whether you want to create a new presentation using the AutoContent Wizard, a design template, or a blank presentation. You can also indicate that you are not creating a new presentation and will instead open an existing presentation.

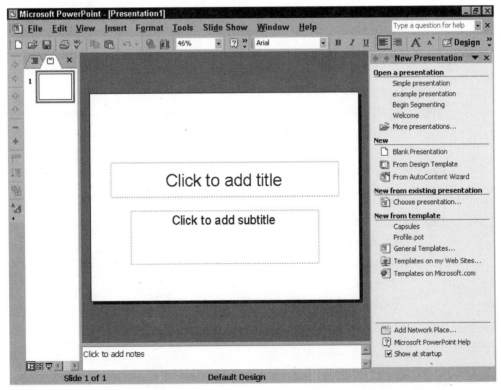

Figure 4-1 The PowerPoint window showing the New Presentation task pane.

To open an existing presentation, you can click one of the Open Presentation hyperlinks. The first four hyperlinks refer to recently opened presentations. The fifth hyperlink, More Presentations, displays an Open dialog box you can use to open any presentation.

If you do indicate that you want to create a new presentation using a design template, PowerPoint replaces the New Presentation task pane with the Slide Design task pane, as shown in Figure 4-2. You can select one of the design templates from the list. When you find the appropriate design template, you can right-click the design template. Then, when PowerPoint displays the Shortcuts menu, choose the Apply To All Slides command to use the design template for every slide in the presentation or choose the Apply To Selected Slides to use the design template for just the selected slide.

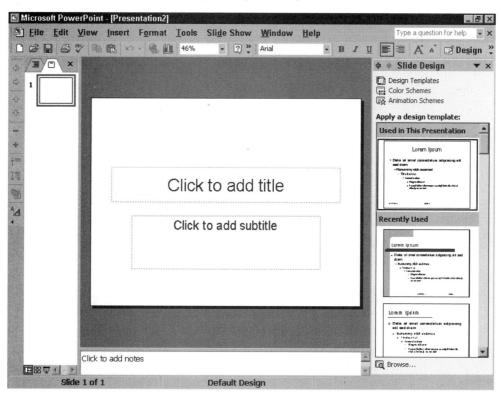

Figure 4-2 The PowerPoint window showing the Slide Design task pane.

Selecting a design template after you start

If you want to use a design template for an existing presentation or you want to change the design template for a presentation, you need to open the presentation—by choosing the File menu's Open command, for example—and then use its Look In box and its unlabeled list box to locate and identify the presentation.

After you open the presentation, you need to display the Slide Design task pane. If the task pane shows, use its Back and Forward buttons to display the Slide Design task pane. If you need to first display the task pane, choose the View menu's Task Pane command. After PowerPoint displays the Slide Design task pane, right-click the design template you want and choose either the Apply To All Slides command or the Apply To Selected Slides command.

NOTE   *PowerPoint stores its design templates in a folder named Presentation Designs. The Presentation Designs folder is a subfolder in the Templates folder. The Templates folder is a folder in whatever folder you chose to install Microsoft Office. Presentation design templates, by the way, use the file type specification .pot.*

Creating your own design templates

Although you will presumably want to work with the design templates already built in or included with the PowerPoint program—after all, these design templates were created by professional artists—you can create your own design template. To do this, you first want to create a presentation that looks just the way you want. (Predictably, that means that you want to perform all sorts of design and formatting tasks that are described in the pages that follow.)

When you do have a presentation that looks exactly the way you want future presentations to look, you can turn this presentation's formatting and design information into a design template. To do this, choose the File menu's Save As command. When PowerPoint displays the Save As dialog box, as shown in Figure 4-3, first use the Save In box to select the folder you've used to store the design templates. As noted, design templates are typically stored in the Presentation Designs subfolder, a folder in the Templates folder, which is in turn a subfolder in the Microsoft Office folder. Next, use the Save As Type list box to indicate that what you want to save is a design template. You can do this by opening the Save As Type box and then choosing the Design Template entry. After you provide this information, you can click the Save button.

Figure 4-3   The Save As dialog box.

After you have created a design template, you can use it in the future by choosing the Format menu's Apply Design Template command.

Customizing the Master Slides

Changing the design template used for a presentation represents the most fundamental customization you can make to the appearance of your presentation. The next most far-reaching change you can make is to the master slides used to create the individual slides in your presentation. A master slide is essentially just a blueprint for creating individual slides.

You can make a variety of changes to a master slide, and thereby to all the slides in your presentation. First, however, you need to display the master slide. To display a master slide, choose the View menu's Master command. When you do this, PowerPoint displays the Master submenu. The Master submenu lists the three types of master slides: Slide Master, Handout Master, and Notes Master. When you are changing the appearance of your presentation, you work with the Slide Master (which specifies how the individual slides in your presentation look).

After you choose the appropriate Master submenu command—presumably the Slide Master command—PowerPoint displays the appropriate master slide. Figure 4-4 shows Slide Master view in the PowerPoint program window. This slide master shows object placeholders and the font styles that are used.

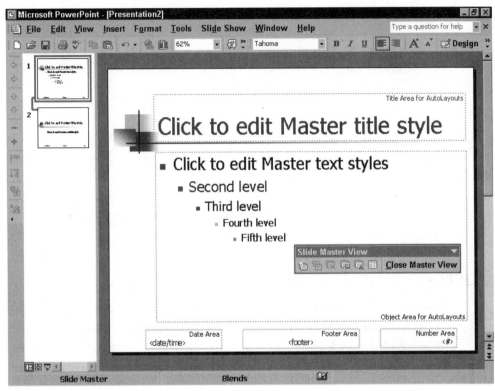

Figure 4-4   Slide Master view.

Changing the background

You can change the background used for each of the slides based on the master slide by simply choosing the Format menu's Background command. When you do, PowerPoint displays the Background dialog box, as shown in Figure 4-5. To choose a background fill for the master slide, open the drop-down list box, which appears in the dialog box. When you do, PowerPoint displays a pop-up box that shows colored background fill options. To select a fill option shown in one of these colored squares, simply click the square.

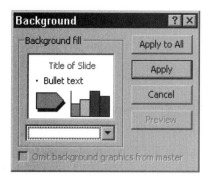

Figure 4-5   The Background dialog box.

When you want to use some other color or pattern besides those shown, you can click either the More Colors command or the Fill Effects command. When you click the More Colors command, PowerPoint displays the Colors dialog box, as shown in Figure 4-6. To use the Colors dialog box, click the color hexagon that uses the color you want.

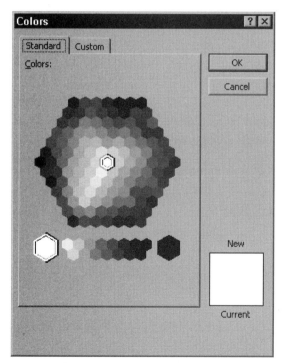

Figure 4-6   The Colors dialog box.

If you choose the Fill Effects command from the list, PowerPoint displays a Fill Effects dialog box, as shown in Figure 4-7. To control background fill, click the

Gradient tab and then use its Colors option buttons, Transparency boxes, Shading Styles option buttons, and Variants buttons to produce the fill effect you want. You can easily experiment with these option buttons and boxes. PowerPoint shows the effect of your color and shading style settings in the Sample box.

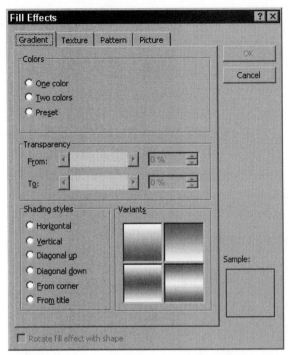

Figure 4-7   The Gradient tab in the Fill Effects dialog box.

The Fill Effects dialog box includes a Texture tab, as shown in Figure 4-8. If you click the Texture tab, PowerPoint displays a collection of boxes that show different textures you can use for the background fill pattern.

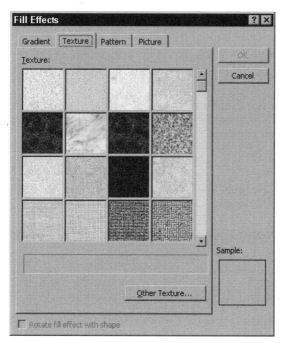

Figure 4-8 The Texture tab in the Fill Effects dialog box.

The Fill Effects dialog box provides a Pattern tab, as shown in Figure 4-9. The Pattern tab works similarly to the Texture tab. You simply click the Pattern box that shows the pattern you want to use. The Pattern tab also includes foreground and background drop-down list boxes. You use these boxes to select the two colors used to create a pattern.

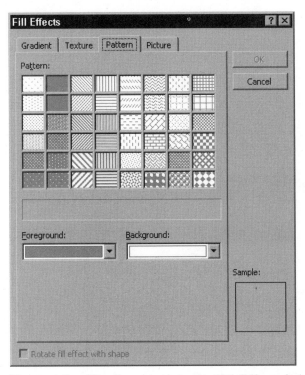

Figure 4-9   The Pattern tab in the Fill Effects dialog box.

The Fill Effects dialog box also provides a Picture tab, which isn't shown in a figure in this step. You can use the Picture tab to insert a picture as the background pattern for your slides. After you've specified the background fill you want to use, you can click the Preview button in the Background dialog box, as shown in Figure 4-5, to see how your background fill pattern looks. If the background fill looks the way you want, click the Apply To All button to change the background pattern of all slides in your presentation.

NOTE   *You can use the Format menu's Background command to change only the background of a single slide or the background of a selected group of slides. To do this, you don't make changes to the master slide background but rather to the slide itself. When you're working with individual slides or sets of slides that are part of a large presentation, you can click the Background dialog box's Apply button. By clicking Apply, PowerPoint applies the background fill change to only the selected slide or slides.*

Changing the color scheme

You can change the color scheme used for a presentation. To do this, first display the Slide Design task pane by clicking the task pane's Back and Forward buttons. (If you need to first display the task pane, choose the View menu's Task Pane command.) Then choose the Color Schemes hyperlink. When you do this, PowerPoint displays the color schemes in the Slide Design task pane, as shown in Figure 4-10.

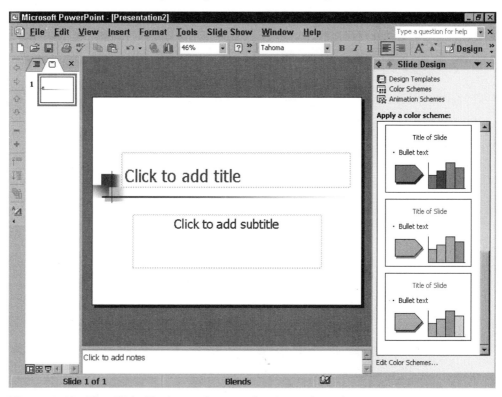

Figure 4-10 The Slide Design task pane showing color schemes.

The Slide Design pane's list of color schemes provides clickable buttons you can use to select an alternative color scheme. Each of these boxes shows the colors these schemes use. After you select the color scheme, right-click the color scheme and choose either the Apply To All Masters or Apply To Selected Masters command from the Shortcuts menu.

Although you probably will work with the color schemes supplied with a design template, you can create your own color scheme. To do this, click the Edit Color Schemes hyperlink shown at the bottom of the Slide Design task pane when it shows color schemes. When you do, PowerPoint displays the Edit Color Scheme dialog box, shown in Figure 4-11.

NOTE   *A color scheme is made up of eight colors: a background color, a text and lines color, a shadows color, a title text color, a fills color, an accent color, an accent and hyperlink color, and an accent and followed hyperlink color.*

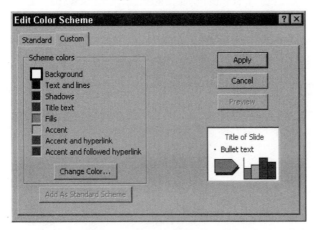

Figure 4-11 The Custom tab in the Edit Color Scheme dialog box.

To change one of these colors, click the color square and then the Change Color button. When you do, PowerPoint displays a Color dialog box like the one shown in Figure 4-12. To pick a color from this dialog box, click the color you want.

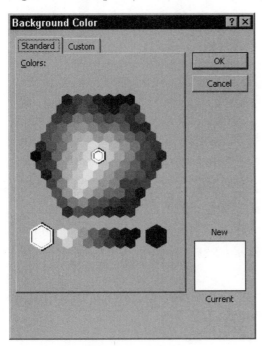

Figure 4-12 The Standard tab in a Color dialog box—in this case, the Background Color dialog box.

If you change the colors in the color scheme, make sure that your colors produce high contrast. To be easy to read, words and pictures on slides need to be bright and clear and contrast strongly with the color of the background. This means two things: First, the ambient light in the room must be subdued enough for the slides to appear bright. Brightness can be achieved with a powerful projector (projectors are rated in lumens; the higher the lumens, the greater the brightness; 600 lumens is a minimum) or by having sufficient darkness in the room or in the end of the room where the slides are being projected. Second, the letters, graphs, and images on each slide must contrast strongly with the selected background color or pattern. Generally, the darker the background color and the lighter the lettering or line color, the greater the contrast and readability.

You can also use this dialog box's Custom tab to select the color you want (see Figure 4-13). You can select a color in two ways: Click a color in the Colors box—the rainbow-colored box you see on the tab—or describe the color using either the Hue, Sat (saturation), or Lum (luminance) set of boxes or the Red, Green, or Blue boxes.

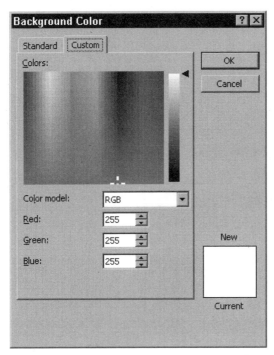

Figure 4-13 The Custom tab in a Color dialog box—in this case, the Background Color dialog box.

To use either set of boxes to describe the color, you enter values into the boxes or use the box's spinner controls. After you pick the color you want to use, click the OK button. PowerPoint returns you to the Custom tab in the Color Scheme box (as shown in Figure 4-11). You might want to make color changes to other colors that make up this scheme. When you are done, click either the Apply button or the Apply To All button.

NOTE   *When you change a master slide, you change all slides that rely on the master slide for design information. You can, however, also change the appearance of individual slides. To do this, you simply display and select the slide you
want to change rather than the master slide. You can also make a change to
some subset of the slides that make up a presentation by using Slide Sorter
view to select the slides you want to change. Slide Sorter view is described in
"Step 6: Prepare Your Presentation."*

Changing text formatting

You can change the font, font style, point size, and other font specifications for the slides in your presentation by using the Format menu's Font command. To use this command, first display the master slide and then click the text object you want to change. After you've done this, choose the appropriate Format menu command or toolbar button.

Changing the font

To change the font for the selected text, choose the Format menu's Font command. PowerPoint displays the Font dialog box, as shown in Figure 4-14.

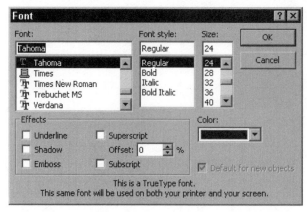

Figure 4-14   The Font dialog box.

To use the Font dialog box, select the font you want from the Font list box. Then choose the font style you want by clicking one of the entries in the Font Style list box: Regular, Bold, Italic, or Bold Italic. Finally, specify the correct point size by entering a point size value in the Size text box or by choosing a point size from the Size list box. (One point equals 1/72 inch.)

TIP   *For easy readability, use large point sizes of bold type that fill your slide with information and convey your message. This means two things. First, don't "worship" white or blank space. White space in itself is not sacred (although many artists think that it is); it should be used to illuminate the text just enough so that your message is communicated strongly. Yes, you should avoid a cluttered look, but make the lettering and images as large as possible so that they fit and read easily. Second, keep type sizes of titles and text equal. PowerPoint templates typically give you a large title (44-point type) and a smaller (32-point) setting for bulleted text. Which is more important on a slide: the title or the content? We think it's the content. Therefore, the font size of the bulleted text should be at least equal to the size of the title. A good way to differentiate titles and text is to have titles on each slide in one color and bulleted or numbered points in other colors.*

You probably won't have an occasion to use them, but the Font dialog box also provides a set of Effects check boxes you can mark to add special effects, such as underlining, shadows, embossing, superscripting, and subscripting.

You can also use a Color drop-down list box to specify what color PowerPoint should use for selected text. This color specification overrides the text color specified for the color scheme—but only for selected text.

TIP   *Use bold lettering. It's not just the height of letters that makes words read far, it's the weight: Fat letters read farther. If you want to fill a room with slides that pack a wallop, choose bold typefaces. Avoid typefaces with serifs, such as Times New Roman. Note that this means that even though PowerPoint uses Times New Roman as its default setting for slides, you still want to use it only in boldface. The tiny serif "feet" on letters disappear from a distance, robbing words of impact. Choose instead Arial Bold or Black or Tahoma Bold or the excellent typeface named Eras (available in font collections and in Corel clip art packages).*

Replacing a font

The Format menu includes a Replace Font command. You can choose this command to display the Replace Font dialog box, as shown in Figure 4-15. It lets you make a wholesale replacement of a font in your presentation. You can use the Replace Font dialog box, for example, to replace every occurrence of the Times New Roman font with the Helvetica font.

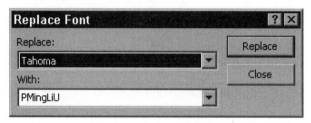

Figure 4-15   The Replace Font dialog box.

Changing text alignment

By default, text is left aligned in text placeholder objects. You can change the alignment used for the selected text object, however, by choosing the Format menu's Alignment command. When you choose this command, PowerPoint displays the Alignment submenu. It lists the four alignment options that are available: Align Left, (which, of course, aligns text left), Center (centers text in the object placeholder), Align Right (right-aligns text), and Justify (stretches out text so that the text is both left- and right-aligned). You can experiment with the Alignment submenu commands to fine-tune the text alignment used on your slides.

Changing the case

The Format menu's Change Case command lets you change the capitalization or case used for the text in the selected text placeholder. You can also use the Change Case command to change the case of just the text that is selected. When you choose the Change Case command, PowerPoint displays the dialog box shown in Figure 4-16. All you do is mark the Option button that corresponds to the capitalization or case rule you want to use.

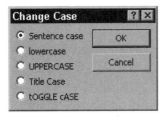

Figure 4-16 The Change Case dialog box.

NOTE   *The Change Case dialog box's option buttons are labeled using words or phrases that show the case for the option.*

Changing the bullets and numbers used for bulleted text

You can change the bullet style that is used or the numbering style used for bulleted or numbered text. To do this, first display the master slide, and then select the bulleted list you want to modify. After you've done this, choose the Format menu's Bullets And Numbering command. When you do, PowerPoint displays the Bullets And Numbering dialog box, as shown in Figure 4-17.

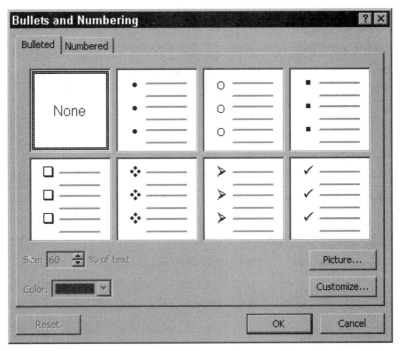

Figure 4-17 The Bulleted tab in the Bullets And Numbering dialog box.

The Size and Color boxes on the Bulleted tab in the Bullets And Numbering dialog box let you specify how large the bullet should be as a percentage of the text size and what color it should be.

To choose a bullet format, simply click the box that uses the bullets you want to use. If none of the boxes shows a bullet you want to use, you might be able to create a superior bullet based on a Wingdings character or an appropriate picture image. To create your own bullet character, click the Customize button. Then, when PowerPoint displays the Bullet dialog box, as shown in Figure 4-18, click the character you want to use. (You might need to first select the Wingdings font or some other appropriate font from the Bullets list box.)

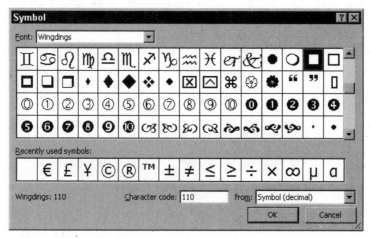

Figure 4-18 The Bullet dialog box.

If you want to use an appropriate picture image for your bullet, you can click the Picture button. When you do, PowerPoint displays a Picture Bullet dialog box (see Figure 4-19). This dialog box lets you view the PowerPoint Clip Art Gallery and select one of its images for use as a bullet.

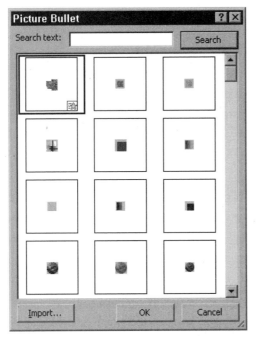

Figure 4-19 The Picture Bullet dialog box.

The Numbered tab in the Bullets And Numbering dialog box, as shown in Figure 4-20, lets you select a numbering style for a bulleted list you've numbered. You simply click the box that shows the numbered text the way you want your slide to look.

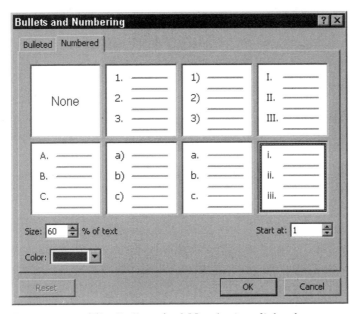

Figure 4-20 The Bullets And Numbering dialog box.

TIP   *When you are displaying a list of information on a slide, you have a choice to precede each listed item with a bullet or a number. Generally, bullets are a writer's tool, and numbers are for speakers. It's easier to say "Number seven" than to have to say "Now look at the seventh bullet." Bullets are fine for a short list, but numbers work better when a natural sequence occurs or you are describing steps or you plan to speak about the separate items on the slide. Numbers also help listeners take notes because they provide a natural index of information.*

Controlling line spacing

You can specify how widely lines of text should be spaced. To do this, select the text object for which you want to specify line spacing, or, if you don't want to do this to an entire text object, select the text by clicking and dragging the mouse. After you've done this, choose the Format menu's Line Spacing command. PowerPoint displays the Line Spacing dialog box, as shown in Figure 4-21.

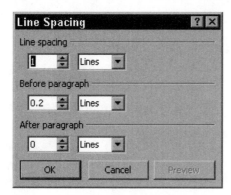

Figure 4-21 The Line Spacing dialog box.

Use the Line Spacing boxes to indicate whether text should be single-spaced, double-spaced, and so on. Use the Before Paragraph box to specify extra lines or whether a portion of an extra line should be placed before a paragraph. Finally, use the After Paragraph box to indicate whether an extra line or portion of a line should be placed after a paragraph.

NOTE   *PowerPoint, like Microsoft Word, views as a paragraph any block of text that ends with you pressing the Enter key. Therefore, a paragraph in PowerPoint is any chunk of text that ends with the Enter key being pressed. Interestingly, pressing the Enter key actually adds to the text a special, hidden symbol called the end-of-paragraph marker.*

Formatting an Object

In addition to the sorts of customization described in the preceding paragraphs, you can change the appearance of most objects you place on PowerPoint slides. In fact, with few exceptions, you can change basically any object you place on a PowerPoint slide. To do this, you simply right-click the object you want to change and choose the Format Placeholder command or the Format AutoShape command from the Shortcuts menu. PowerPoint displays a Format dialog box (the name varies depending on what you right-clicked) that looks like the one shown in Figure 4-22.

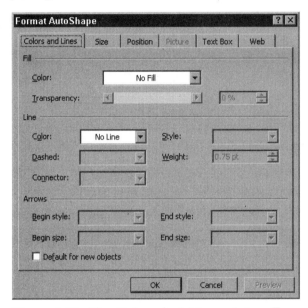

Figure 4-22 The Colors And Lines tab in a Format dialog box—in this case, Format AutoShape.

The Format dialog box generally includes a Colors And Lines tab that lets you specify the fill color that should be used for the object or placeholder. The tab also includes a set of line boxes that let you choose the line color, the line style, and its weight as a point size for any lines used in the object or placeholder. Finally, if what you selected is an arrow or a line, you might be able to use the arrow boxes to control the appearance or specify the appearance of the line.

The Format dialog box also typically includes a Size tab, as shown in Figure 4-23. This tab generally lets you size an object by providing its height and width. You can also use the Size tab to rotate an object by entering a value in the Rotation box. If you want, you can even scale the object or resize its original dimensions by using the Scale Height and Scale Width boxes. To use these boxes, you enter the percentage of the original size you want the newly rescaled image to be.

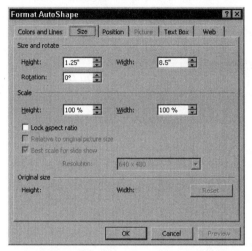

Figure 4-23 The Size tab in a format dialog box—in this case, Format AutoShape.

The Format dialog box also provides other tabs you can use to control or change the appearance of some object or placeholder:

- The Position tab, for example, lets you specify the object location of the object using text boxes and drop-down list boxes.

- The Picture tab lets you crop a picture image and make modest changes to the image's color, brightness, and contrast.

- The Text Box tab lets you specify how text should be anchored inside a text place-holder box and what internal margins PowerPoint should use for positioning text inside the placeholder. The Text Box tab also provides check boxes you can use to tell PowerPoint how it should wrap text inside the placeholder, resize the placeholder if the text is too large to fit, and even rotate text inside a placeholder.

- The Web tab lets you specify some text replacement for a graphics object. You use the Web tab when you are publishing a PowerPoint presentation on the Web. By specifying a text replacement for an object, you give someone who doesn't have a Web browser capable of displaying graphic images the chance to still be able to see your presentation's information.

TIP   *To make your slides look just right, take advantage of an optical illusion: Our eyes want to see the horizontal center of a page 5 percent above the actual measured center. This is the* visual, *or* optical, *center of a page. Therefore, always allow more blank space to show at the bottom of slides, beneath the text, than you allow at the top, above the title. If you place lettering all the way to the bottom of a slide, it will look heavy, as though it's falling off the slide. So "lift" your text, and your slides will satisfy people's aesthetic sense.*

Working with Special Placeholders

If you display a master slide, you'll notice that PowerPoint provides placeholders to provide date and time information and a slide number near the bottom of each slide. You'll probably want to use this information on your slides, but if you don't, you can delete any of these items by clicking the appropriate placeholder to select it and then using the Edit menu's Clear command.

Using the Formatting Toolbar

There isn't much reason to spend lots of time talking about the Formatting toolbar, but let's just quickly mention this much: After you've become comfortable working with the Format menu command, particularly the Format menu's Font command and the Bullets And Numbering command, you will want to explore the tools provided by the Formatting toolbar, as shown in Figure 4-24.

Figure 4-24 The Formatting toolbar.

NOTE   *Figure 4-25 shows a picture of a free-floating toolbar to make it easy to see,*
but typically the Formatting toolbar is anchored just below the menu bar.

The Formatting toolbar provides several boxes and numerous clickable buttons you can use to, in effect, quickly choose some formatting option. For example, if you select some text and click the button with the large *B* on it, you have boldfaced the selected text. Other Formatting toolbar buttons let you make further specifications, control text alignment, and change text into a bulleted or numbered list, for example. You won't have any problem figuring out what various buttons do by experimenting to see their effect. If you make a mistake or use a button that has an effect you don't want to keep, simply click the Undo button, which appears on the Standard toolbar.

Step 5

ADD SPECIAL EFFECTS

Featuring:

- Using Special Slide Transitions
- Animating Slide Text
- Controlling Text Animation
- Selecting a custom Animation Effect
- Adding Sounds and Movies

One of the most interesting and controversial features of PowerPoint is the special effects it lets you add to slides. You can use special slide-to-slide transitions, animation, sound effects, and even multimedia objects, like video clips, to enhance and enrich your presentations. Admittedly, these special effects are often overused and overdone, but the tools are also appropriate and useful for many presentations. Accordingly, this step explains how to use the them.

Using Special Slide Transitions

If you don't specify otherwise, PowerPoint simply displays the next slide. In other words, PowerPoint uses no fancy or noticeable slide-to-slide transition. You can, however, specify that PowerPoint should use a slide-to-slide transition. To do so, take the following steps:

1. Display the presentation using Slide Sorter view.

To display the open presentation using Slide Sorter view, choose the View menu's Slide Sorter command. When you do, PowerPoint displays the presentation's slides using Slide Sorter view, as shown in Figure 5-1.

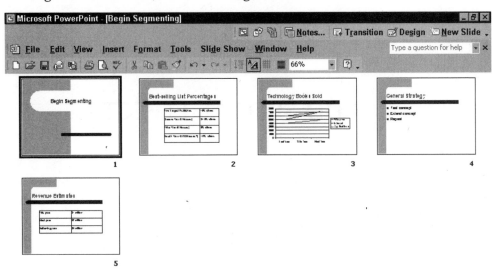

Figure 5-1   Slide Sorter view.

2. Indicate that you want to use a slide transition.

To indicate you want to use a slide transition, click the Slide Transition button. When you do, PowerPoint displays the Slide Transition task pane, as shown in Figure 5-2.

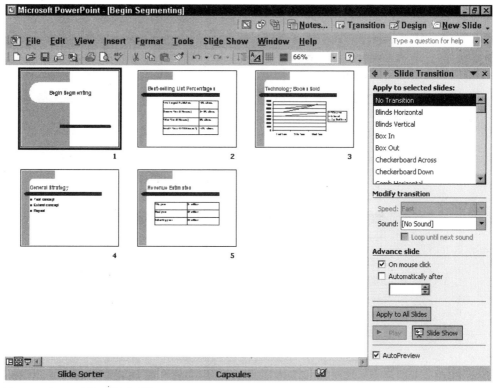

Figure 5-2 The Slide Transition task pane.

3. Choose the transition effect.

You use the Apply To Selected Slides list in the Slide Transition task pane to choose the transition effect you want. You can choose from more than fifty different slide-to-slide transition effects, so you'll need to do some exploration to find which one you will want to use. When you've chosen an effect, use the Speed list box to indicate how quickly (Slow, Medium, or Fast) PowerPoint should perform the effect.

NOTE *When you choose an effect from the drop-down list box, PowerPoint uses the Preview area, also shown in the Effect area, to show you what the effect looks like.*

4. (Optional) Choose a sound.

If you want to also have PowerPoint play a sound as part of the slide transition, select the sound from the Sound drop-down list box. PowerPoint provides several sounds you can choose: Applause, [Breaking] Glass, Gunshot, and Laser, for example.

You can also choose the Other Sound entry from the Sound drop-down list box. If you do, PowerPoint displays the Add Sound dialog box, as shown in Figure 5-3. You can use the Add Sound dialog box to choose some other sound for the transition. To use the Add Sound dialog box, first specify the location of the sound file using the Look In drop-down list box. Then, double-click the sound file from the list of files displayed in the list box area.

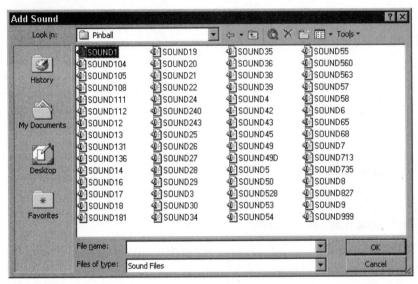

Figure 5-3   The Add Sound dialog box.

NOTE   *Later in this step, in the "Adding Sounds and Movies" section, we'll describe the other ways you can add sound to your presentation.*

5. Tell PowerPoint what triggers the transition.

You use the Advance Slide check boxes to tell PowerPoint what event should trigger or start the slide-to-slide transition.

* If you want PowerPoint to transition to the next slide when you click the mouse or press the space bar, mark the On Mouse Click check box.

* If you want to automatically transition to the next slide, mark the Automatically After check box and enter the number of seconds that PowerPoint should show the slide.

Animating Slide Text

You can add movement, or *animation*, to text. In fact, this will probably be the most common animation you use for your presentations.

NOTE   *Later in this step, in the "Selecting a Custom Animation Effect" section, we'll also describe how to animate other objects on a slide.*

Animating title and slide text

PowerPoint provides animation schemes for animating slides. To use these animation schemes, display the Slide Design task pane (you may need to click the Back and Forward buttons) and then click the Animation Schemes hyperlink. When you do, PowerPoint displays the Slide Design task pane shown in Figure 5-4.

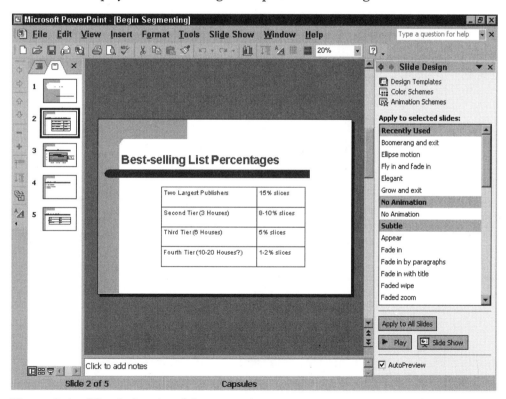

Figure 5-4   The Animation Schemes options.

To add animation to your presentation, select the slides you want to animate. Then, select an animation scheme from the list box.

When you select an animation scheme, PowerPoint illustrates the animation effects for the selected slides. You can also click the Play button, which appears near the bottom of the Slide Design task pane, to see the animation effects.

NOTE   *To apply the selected animation scheme to all the slides in a presentation— not just the selected slides—click the Apply To All Slides button.*

Controlling Text Animation

The animation schemes available through the Slide Design task page, described in the preceding paragraphs, let you turn on text animation, and that might be all you want to do. However, the Custom Animation task pane, shown in Figure 5-5, lets you control the way text animation works.

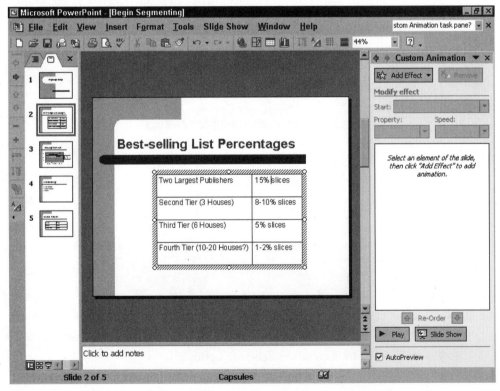

Figure 5-5   The PowerPoint window showing the Custom Animation task pane.

Selecting a custom animation effect

The Custom Animation task pane lets you describe what special effects should occur for a slide item you've animated. You can tell PowerPoint to add four types of animation to a slide item:

- Entrance animation, which is movement that occurs as an item is added to the slide.

- Emphasis animation, which is movement that occurs while the item is on the slide.

- Exit animation, which is movement that occurs as an item is removed from the slide.

- Motion path animation, which specifies where and how slide items move as they move.

To add entrance animation to a slide item, select the item, click the Add Effect button and choose the Entrance command. When PowerPoint displays the Entrance submenu, choose the entrance animation effect you want to use when PowerPoint displays the item: Blinds, Box, Checkerboard, Diamond, or Fly In. If none of these entry effects is what you want, you can choose the More Effects command to display the Add Entrance Effect dialog box, as shown in Figure 5-6. To use one of its entrance effects, click the button that describes the effect.

Figure 5-6   The Add Entrance Effect dialog box.

If you have a question about how some animation effect works, just add the effect. PowerPoint shows the effect as you add it and places the new effect on the list shown in the Custom Animation task pane. If you don't like the newly added effect, select it from the Custom Animation task pane and click the Remove button.

To add emphasis animation to a slide item, select the item, click the Add Effect button and choose the Emphasis command. When PowerPoint displays the Emphasis submenu, choose the emphasis animation effect you want to use when PowerPoint displays the item: Change Font, Change Font Size, Change Font Style, Grow/Shrink, or Spin. If none of these emphasis effects is what you want, you can choose the More Effects command to display the Add Emphasis Effect dialog box, as shown in Figure 5-7. To use one of its entrance effects, click the button that describes the effect.

Figure 5-7   The Add Emphasis Effect dialog box.

To add exit animation to a slide item, select the item, click the Add Effect button and choose the Exit command. When PowerPoint displays the Exit submenu, choose the entry animation effect you want to use when PowerPoint finishes displaying the item:

Blinds, Box, Checkerboard, Diamond, or Fly In. (These are the same choices you have for entrance animation.) Again, if none of these entry effects is what you want, you can choose the More Effects command to display the Add Exit Effect dialog box, as shown in Figure 5-8. To use one of its exit effects, click the button that describes the effect.

Figure 5-8   The Add Exit Effect dialog box.

To specify how an item should move when it moves, select the item, click the Add Effect button and choose the Motion Path command. When PowerPoint displays the Motion Path submenu, choose the motion path effect you want PowerPoint to use: 5 Point Star, Curvy Star, Diamond, Heart, Hexagon, or Loop De Loop. If none of these motion paths is what you want, you can choose the Draw Custom Path command to display another submenu of commands (Line, Curve, Freeform, and Scribble) that actually let you manually draw the motion path you want. Or, you can choose the More Motion Paths command to display the Add Motion Path dialog box, as shown in Figure 5-9. To use one of its motion paths, click the button that describes the path.

Figure 5-9   The Add Motion Path dialog box.

NOTE   *To review your all animation effects once you have finished adding them, click the Play button to play the animation effects for the active slide or click the Slide Show to show the entire set of slides including their animation effects.*

Specifying the order of text animation effects

You should consider one other useful point concerning animation: PowerPoint animates individual objects. This means that you might have several objects on a slide that are all animated.

Be default, PowerPoint plays these animation effects in the same order as you added the animation to the slide. You can change this order by using the animation effects list box, which also appears on the Custom Animation task pane. This list box lists animation effects in the order they occur. To change a particular effect's place on the list, click the effect and then move it by clicking the Reorder buttons.

Fine-tuning an animation effect

The Custom Animation task pane provides three other boxes for fine-tuning how an animation effect occurs. For example, the Custom Animation task pane provides a Start box that lets you indicate whether the animation effect should start when you click the slide, should start simultaneous with the previous effect, or should start after the previous effect.

The Custom Animation task pane also provides other boxes for controlling other animation effects. Which boxes you see depend on what sort of animation effect you're fine-tuning. If you're fine-tuning the way slide text is moved onto the slide, for example, PowerPoint provides Direction and Speed boxes you use to specify the direction from which the slide text is moved and the speed with which the slide text is moved. If you've told PowerPoint to change the font used for text as an emphasis effect, PowerPoint provides Font and Duration boxes you use to choose the new font and specify how long it is to be displayed.

To learn how any of these boxes work, you can experiment. After you select an animation effect, as mentioned earlier, PowerPoint shows what the effect does. You can also click the Play button to replay all the animation effects for the slide.

Controlling the timing of animation

If you right-click an animation effect listed on the Custom Animation task pane and choose the Timing command from the Shortcuts menu, PowerPoint displays the Timing tab of the effect's options dialog box, as shown in Figure 5-10. The Timing tab lets you control how quickly the animation occurs.

The Delay box lets you specify a delay before the animation starts. The Speed box lets you spectfy how long an animation takes. The Repeat box lets you specify how many times an effect should be repeated. The Triggers command button adds buttons to the Timing tab that let you specfy how mouse clicks control the animation.

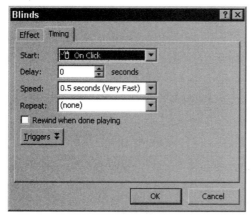

Figure 5-10 The Timing tab.

Customizing animation effects

If you right-click an animation effect listed on the Custom Animation task pane and choose the Effects Options command from the Shortcuts menu, PowerPoint displays the Effect tab of the effect's options dialog box, as shown in Figure 5-11. The Effect tab's lets you further control the actual animation or movement used for a slide.

Typically, you can add sound to an animation effect using the Sound box on the Effect tab. Depending on the animation effect you're customizing, you may also have options such as describing what should happen after the animation and whether text should be animated letter-by-letter or word-by-word.

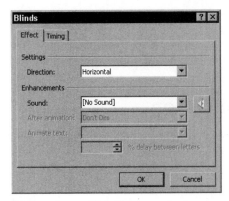

Figure 5-11 The Effects tab.

Adding Sounds and Movies

PowerPoint lets you add both sounds and movies to your slides. Interestingly, PowerPoint also comes with sound files and several movies (they are motion clips based on animated gif files) in its Clip Gallery.

NOTE   *An animated gif file is an image file that shows movement. You commonly see animated gif images on web pages.*

Adding sound

To add sound to a PowerPoint slide, you either choose a sound from the PowerPoint Clip Gallery or insert a sound file stored somewhere else on your computer.

Using a sound from the Clip Gallery

To insert or use a sound from the PowerPoint Clip Gallery, follow these steps:

1. **Choose the Sound From Media Gallery command.**

To choose the Sound From Media Gallery command, first choose the Insert menu's Movies And Sounds command. Then, when PowerPoint displays the Movies And Sounds submenu, choose its Sound From Media Gallery command. PowerPoint displays the Insert Clip Art task pane, as shown in Figure 5-12.

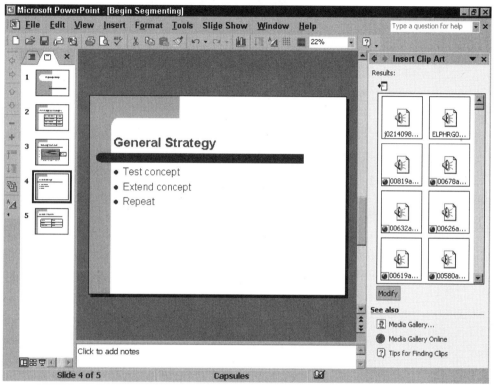

Figure 5-12 The Insert Clip Art task pane.

2. **Find the sound you want.**

You use the list box in the Insert Clip Art task pane to locate the sound you want. Or, you can click the Media Gallery hyperlink and then use the Media Gallery window to locate the sound you want.

3. **Play the clip.**

To check a clip, right-click the sound and choose the Preview/Properties command. PowerPoint plays the sound and opens the Preview/Properties dialog box, as shown in Figure 5-13.

Figure 5-13   The Preview/Properties dialog box.

4. Insert the sound.

When you locate the sound you want, right-click the sound and choose Insert from the Shortcuts menu. When you do, PowerPoint inserts the sound on the open or selected slide.

5. Specify when the sound should be played.

When you choose the Insert command, you'll see a Message box like the one shown in Figure 5-14. PowerPoint displays this Message box to ask you when you want a sound played. If you want the sound to play automatically when you display this slide in your presentation, click the Yes button. If you don't want the sound to play automatically, click the No button. If you click the No button, you need to click the Sound File icon on the slide in order to play it.

Figure 5-14   The Message box that asks when you want the sound played.

Using a sound file

You can also insert a sound that is stored on your computer or network in a sound file. To do this, you need to know the sound file's name and its folder location. Assuming that you do have this information, you insert a sound file by taking the following steps:

1. Choose the Sound From File command.

To choose the Sound From File command, first choose the Insert menu's Movies And Sounds command. When PowerPoint displays the Movies And Sounds submenu, choose its Sound From File command. PowerPoint displays the Insert Sound dialog box, as shown in Figure 5-15.

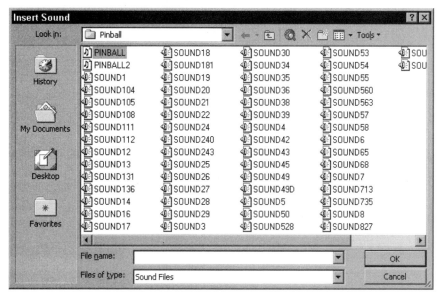

Figure 5-15 The Insert Sound dialog box.

2. Find the sound.

Use the Look In box to select the folder that holds the sound file. If the sound is really in a subfolder or in a sub-subfolder, you might need to first select and open the parent folder.

TIP   *To play a sound listed in the Insert Sound dialog box, right-click the sound and choose Play from the Shortcuts menu.*

3. Insert the sound.

When you've found the folder with the sound, double-click the sound file to insert the sound on your slide.

When you do this, PowerPoint closes the Insert Sound dialog box. Beneath the Insert Sound dialog box, PowerPoint displays a Message box just like the one shown in Figure 5-15. It asks whether you want your sound to play automatically when the slide is displayed. If you do, click Yes. If you don't, click No. (If you do click No, you play the sound by clicking its icon, which will appear on the slide.)

Recording your own sound file

The Movies And Sounds submenu also displays a Record Sound command. If your computer has a microphone, you can use the Record Sound command to start a small Sound Recorder program, as shown in Figure 5-16. The Record Sound command lets you record sounds using your computer's microphone, and it works just like a simple tape recorder. After you record a sound and save it as a file to your computer's hard disk, you can insert the sound onto a slide, as described in the preceding sequence of numbered steps.

Figure 5-16 The Record Sound dialog box.

Adding movies

You can add motion clips or video clips to your slides. This process resembles closely the process used to add sound clips to your slides.

Using a motion clip from the Clip Gallery

To add a motion clip to your slide using the Movie Clip Gallery, take the following steps:

1. **Choose the Movie From Media Gallery command.**

   To choose the Movie From Media Gallery command, first choose the Insert menu's Movies And Sounds command. Then, when PowerPoint displays the Movies And Sounds submenu, choose its Movie From Media Gallery command. PowerPoint displays the Insert Clip Art task pane.

2. **Find the motion clip you want.**

   You use the list box in the Insert Clip Art task pane to locate the motion clip you want to use on a PowerPoint slide. Or, you can click the Media Gallery hyperlink and then use the Media Gallery window to locate the motion clip you want.

3. **Play the motion clip.**

   To check a clip, right-click it and choose Preview/Properties from the Shortcuts menu.

4. Insert the motion clip.

To insert the motion clip, right-click it and choose Insert. When you do, PowerPoint inserts the motion clip on the open or selected slide.

Using a motion clip file

To insert a motion or video clip stored as a file on your computer, take the following steps:

1. Choose the Motion From File command.

To choose the Motion From File command, first choose the Insert menu's Movies And Sounds command. When PowerPoint displays the Movies And Sounds submenu, choose its Movies From File command. When you do, PowerPoint displays the Insert Movie dialog box, as shown in Figure 5-17.

Figure 5-17 The Insert Movie dialog box.

2. Find the motion clip or video clip you want to use.

Use the Look In box to select the folder that holds the movie file. If the movie is really in a subfolder or a sub-subfolder, you might need to first select and open the parent folder.

3. Find the motion clip or video clip you want to use.

After you've found the folder with the movie, double-click the movie file to insert the movie onto your slide.

When you do this, PowerPoint closes the Insert Movie dialog box. Beneath the Insert Movie dialog box, PowerPoint displays a Message box, as shown in Figure 5-18, that asks whether you want your movie to play automatically when the slide is displayed. If you do, click Yes. If you don't, click No. If you do click No, it means that you will have to play the movie by clicking it.

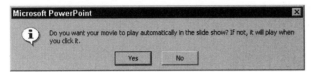

Figure 5-18 The Message box that asks when you want the movie shown.

Customizing your multimedia effects

You can exert significant control over the way PowerPoint handles any multimedia objects you place on a PowerPoint slide. To do this, right-click the multimedia object and then choose the Custom Animation command from the Shortcuts menu. When PowerPoint displays the Custom Animation task pane, right-click the animation effect and choose Effect Options from the Shortcuts menu. PowerPoint displays a dialog box like the one shown in Figure 5-19.

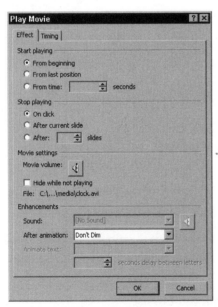

Figure 5-19 The Play Movie dialog box showing the Effect tab.

Controlling When a Multimedia Object's Animation Starts

The Start Playing buttons—From Beginning, From Last Position, and From Time—let you specify when a multimedia object starts playing. Mark the From Beginning button if you want the multimedia object to play from the start of the movie or sound. Mark the Last Position button if you want the multimedia object to start playing where it last stopped playing. Mark the From Time button if you want to start playing a movie or sound a specified number of seconds after the movie or sound begins. If you do mark the From Time button, you also need to provide the number of seconds using the Seconds box.

The Stop Playing buttons—On Click, After Current Slide, and After [X] Slides—let you specify when the multimedia object stops playing. Mark the On Click button to stop playing a multimedia effect when the presenter clicks the object. Mark the After Current Slide button if you want to stop playing the multimedia object when you stop displaying the slide with the object. Mark the After [X] Slides button if you want to stop playing the multimedia object after a specified number of slides. If you do mark the After [X] Slides button, you also need to provide the number of slides during which the multimedia object should play using the Slides box.

The Movie Settings button and box let you set the movie sound volume and hide the movie object icon when the movie isn't playing. To adjust the movie volume, click the Movie Volume button and drag the volume slider control that appears up or down. To tell PowerPoint it shouldn't display the movie object when the movie isn't playing, check the Hide While Not Playing box.

NOTE   *If you're adjusting the effects for a sound multimedia object, PowerPoint replaces the Movie Settings button and box with the Sound Settings button and box. The Sound options, however, work like the Movie options.*

The Enhancements boxes let you augment a multimedia object's animation or sound effects. The Sound box, for example, lets you tell PowerPoint it should play a sound while the animation effect occurs. The After Animation box lets you tell PowerPoint that it should dim or hide or camouflage in some other way the multimedia object after playing. The Animate Text boxes let you fine-tune the way that any textual animation works.

NOTE   *Not all multimedia objects can be customized. If you insert animated gif images on a slide, for example, you might not be able to make any changes to their animation.*

Adding sound from a music CD

You can also play a CD track during a presentation. To do this, you need, predictably, the CD in your computer's CD drive or DVD drive.

To play a sound or track from a CD, choose the Insert menu's Movies And Sounds command. Then choose the Play CD Audio Track command from the Movies And Sounds menu. When you choose this command, PowerPoint displays the Movie And Sound Options dialog box, as shown in Figure 5-20. Use the Play CD Audio Track Start boxes to enter the track number of the first track you want to play and the Play CD Audio Track End boxes to enter the track number of the last track you want to play. If you want to play only one track, enter the same number into both boxes.

Figure 5-20 The Movie And Sound Options dialog box.

If you want to play only a portion of the track, you can also enter the starting times in the Start At box and the ending times in the End At boxes. Using the Start At and End At boxes means, of course, that you need to know the exact time the portion of the track you want to listen to starts and ends.

If you want to have the track continue to replay, you can check the Loop Until Stopped box. The Loop Until Stopped box appears near the top of the Movie And Sound Options dialog box in the Play Options area.

Step 6

PREPARE YOUR PRESENTATION

Featuring:

- Reviewing Your Presentation
- Creating Speaker's Notes
- Rehearsing Your Presentation
- Setting Up Your Presentation
- Using the Pack And Go Wizard

After you create your PowerPoint presentation by doing the things described in the preceding pages of this book, you still need to prepare for the actual presentation you'll make by standing in front of an audience. Fortunately, preparing your presentation after you've constructed the actual slides isn't difficult. You want to review the slides in your presentation, draft any speaker's notes you'll use as you present the slides, and prepare any handout materials you'll need for presentation aids. How you accomplish this work is described in the paragraphs that follow.

Reviewing Your Presentation

After you create the slides that make up your presentation, you'll want to review them. You can do this in either of two ways. You can use Slide Sorter view, which is the equivalent of an onscreen light table that lets you see, at the same time, each of the slides in your presentation and their order. Or, you can show the presentation slide-by-slide—seeing onscreen what your audience will later see in the actual presentation.

Using Slide Sorter view

To use Slide Sorter view, first open the presentation you want to review, and then choose the View menu's Slide Sorter command. PowerPoint displays Slide Sorter view, as shown in Figure 6-1.

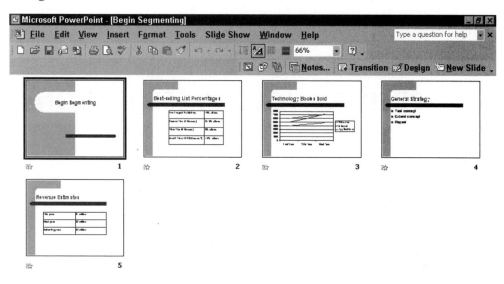

Figure 6-1 Slide Sorter view.

Slide Sorter view displays each of the slides in your presentation, although in miniaturized versions. You can also verify that their order is correct and, if necessary, change their order.

NOTE *The Zoom box on the Standard toolbar lets you control how large the slides shown in Slide Sorter view appear. If you want to see bigger pictures of these slides, enter a larger percentage in the Zoom box. If you enter a very large value in the Zoom box, the slides will probably get too large to all appear in the window at one time, but you can still scroll up and down to see them.*

You can use Slide Sorter view to reorganize your presentation's slides:

- To move a slide to a new position, click the slide and then drag it to the new location you want to use. When you release the mouse button, PowerPoint moves the slide to its new position.

- To delete a slide from the presentation, click the slide and then choose the Edit menu's Delete Slide command or press the Delete key.

- To remove a slide without actually deleting it, right-click the slide so that PowerPoint displays the Shortcuts menu. Then choose its Hide Slide command. To identify a hidden slide, PowerPoint draws an X through the slide's number. The slide's number appears beneath the lower right corner of the slide. To unhide the slide, right-click the slide and choose the Shortcuts menu's Hide Slide command again.

You can also use the Slide Sorter window to review the slide-to-slide transitions and slide animations. Below the left lower corner of each slide, PowerPoint provides two small, clickable buttons. Click the first button to see the slide-to-slide transition. Click the second button to see any animation you're using on the slide.

Running through the presentation

You can also quickly run through the presentation at your own computer in order to review it. To run your presentation, choose the View menu's Slide Show command. When you do, PowerPoint displays the first slide in your presentation using the full screen, as shown in Figure 6-2. PowerPoint will use any animation or special effects you've specified, too.

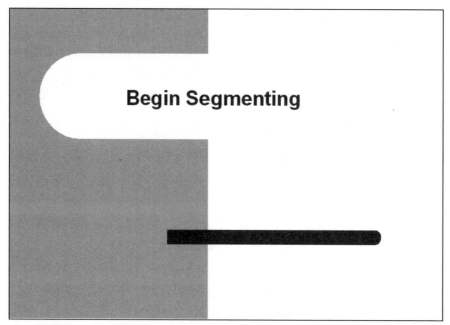

Figure 6-2   A picture of a first presentation slide.

To move through your presentation, you simply display the next slide. Assuming that you are manually controlling the movement through the presentation's slides, either click the mouse or press the spacebar. If you want to play a movie or sound that requires manual interaction or triggering, point to the object that represents the movie or sound.

You can use the left- and right-arrow keys to move forward and backward in a presentation. Pressing the left-arrow key tells PowerPoint to either display the previous slide or undo the previous animation. Pressing the right-arrow key tells PowerPoint to either display the next slide or perform the next animation.

NOTE   *Clicking the mouse or pressing the spacebar, the right-arrow key or left-arrow key only does the next bit of slide movement or undoes the last bit. This might be a piece of animation that moves something onto the slide, or it might be the display of the slide itself.*

When you get to the end of the slides, PowerPoint displays a blank or black slide. At the top of the slide, PowerPoint displays in small type the message "End of slide show, click to exit." To finish the slide show, click the screen, press the space bar, or press the Escape key. PowerPoint redisplays the PowerPoint program window using the same view it used before you started the slide show.

Creating Speaker's Notes

After you've reviewed and tested your presentation, you might want to create speaker's notes.

Drafting speaker's notes

The easiest way to collect speaker's notes is by using the Speaker's Notes pane, which PowerPoint provides in Normal view. Figure 6-3, for example, shows a simple presentation displayed using Normal view. Along the left edge of the PowerPoint Presentation window, the presentation outline appears. In the major part of the window, PowerPoint shows a picture of the selected slide. Beneath this slide, however, PowerPoint displays a small pane. You can use this Speaker's Notes pane to enter any notes you want to use as you talk about the selected or displayed slide.

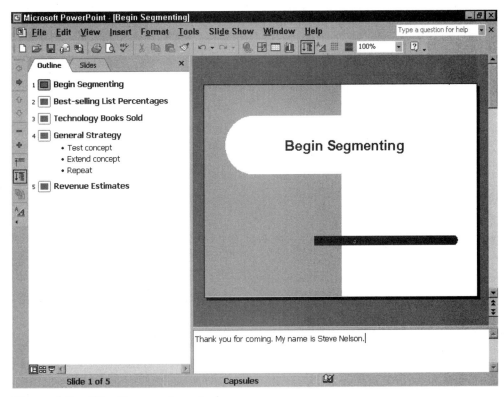

Figure 6-3   The Presentation window.

To enter your speaker's notes, take the following steps:

1. **Display Normal view for the presentation.**

   Open the presentation if necessary, and then choose the View menu's Normal command. PowerPoint displays a Presentation window, as shown in Figure 6-3.

2. **Select the first slide in your presentation.**

   To begin adding speaker's notes, first click the title slide in your presentation.

3. **Enter your welcoming comments or introductory remarks.**

   With the first title slide selected and displayed, click the Speaker's Notes pane. PowerPoint places the insertion point cursor at the beginning of the pane. Now type whatever remarks you want to use for starting your presentation. You might want to type complete text or simply the bulleted points you want to make as you begin your presentation.

4. **Create speaker's notes for the other slides in your presentation.**

   Click the next slide without speaker's notes. After PowerPoint shows that slide in the Slide pane, use the Speaker's Notes pane to record what you want to say when that slide is displayed. Again, all you need to do is click the Speaker's Notes pane and then type.

   When you complete the speaker's notes for one slide, repeat this same process to add speaker's notes to subsequent slides.

NOTE *All the same text-entry and text-editing techniques that work in the Outline pane also work in the Speaker's Notes pane.*

Planning your speaker's notes

As you plan what you want to say, consider taking three steps to make sure you present relevant, interesting information:

1. **Study your audience.**

   Identify to whom you will be speaking. A good way to do this is to consider what *role* they will be playing as they listen: Are they listening as members of a safety committee? As customers? As your sales staff? As shareholders or stakeholders? As members of a professional association? What do you think the audience wants to do with the information you'll present? Address the audience in the role they are playing as they listen to you. To do so, it helps to find out (ask a person who will be in the audience in advance or ask the person who invites you to speak) or figure out (by using your intuition or knowledge of the group) the audience's wants, worries, and wonders. For example, what information about your topic do they want to hear so that they can make intelligent decisions, meet their goals, or achieve their dreams? What information don't they want to hear because they already know it, or they have absolutely no interest in the topic? What problems do audience members wrestle with? What are they afraid of in relation to your topic? What do they most want to know?

2. **Determine your purpose.**

When you finish speaking, what's the one main response you want the audience to make? What specific points do you want them to remember, understand, or be aware of? Or, what one (or more) specific action(s) do you want them to take (and what steps should they take first)? When should they act (deadline or frequency)?

3. **Determine your message.**

If the audience forgets everything else you say, what is the one point you want them to remember, believe, or do? Can you express this in one complete sentence, or in a 9-second, 25-word (or less) sound bite? Can you summarize your entire message, theme, or suggestion in one sentence, or in one word? Lawyers often use a one-word technique with their opening argument to the jury: "Jealousy. This trial is going to be all about jealousy," thereby planting a seed in the minds of the jury. Audiences enjoy crisp, clear statements they can remember or be inspired to act upon.

Writing your speaker's notes

If you want a great way to write speaker notes

or to prepare a complete written speech—

one that is easy to read from—

try the format you're reading right now.

Instead of writing long paragraphs,

which are easy to get lost in,

write separate lines as you see here.

Include one idea per line.

Each line ends with a pause and a breath.

For easier reading,

experiment with lines set space-and-a-half or double-space.

Make the typeface as large and bold as possible,

so the words can be easily read from belt high.

Mark the key words in each line with a highlighter,

so you can emphasize your ideas.

To read with complete eye contact,

try this technique after you've written and rehearsed the lines.

Glance down at line one and put it in your short-term memory.

Lift your eyes and speak the words looking into someone's eyes.

Glance down at line two and record it in your memory.

Lift your eyes again and say the words into someone else's eyes.

Repeat this process for maximum eye contact.

To connect with your audience when you speak,

remember to spend most of your time looking at people's eyes,

not at your notes or at your slides.

Reviewing your speaker's notes

After you've created your speaker's notes, you will probably want to print a hard copy. This might make reviewing them easier. (The onscreen pane is rather small—even if you resize it.) You'll also eventually want to have, of course, a printed hard copy of the speaker's notes to use as a reference when you make your presentation.

To print your speaker's notes, simply choose the File menu's Print command. When PowerPoint displays the Print dialog box, as shown in Figure 6-4, open the Print What list box and select the Notes Pages entry. Then click OK. PowerPoint prints each slide and each slide's speaker's notes on a single piece of paper. The printed notes pages then become a handy tool for both reviewing your speaker's notes and perhaps for later actually making your presentation.

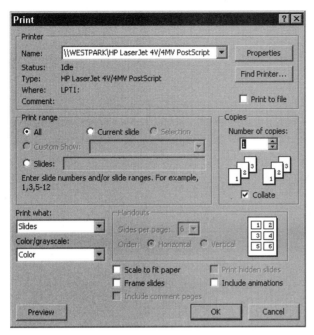

Figure 6-4   The Print dialog box.

Rehearsing Your Presentation

After you've created your speaker's notes and printed a copy of the notes pages as a reference, you will probably want to rehearse your presentation. PowerPoint, fortunately, includes a handy tool you can use to do this. To rehearse your presentation, including and perhaps especially the spoken part, open the presentation file you want to rehearse. Then choose the Slide Show menu's Rehearse Timings command.

Using the Rehearsal Timing window

When you choose this command, PowerPoint starts the slide show and also displays a Rehearsal Timing window you can use to time your presentation. Figure 6-5 shows the way your screen looks. The main part of the screen simply displays a slide from your presentation. In the upper left corner of the screen, as shown in Figure 6-5, you can see a small Rehearsal Timing window. This Rehearsal Timing window includes two timers—one that shows the time you've spent on that slide and one that shows the amount of time you've already spent on the presentation. The Rehearsal Timing window also includes a Pause button you can click to stop your rehearsal and the timer, a Next button you can use to move to the next slide, and a Repeat button you can use to restart the rehearsal timing.

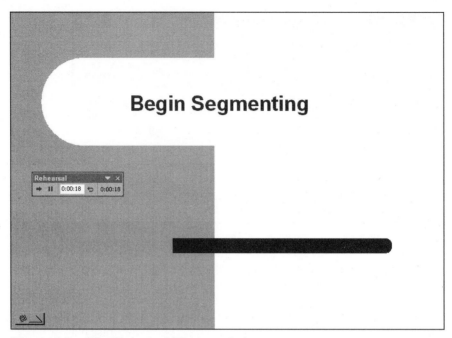

Figure 6-5 The Rehearsal Timing window.

To rehearse your presentation, simply say whatever you want to say about a slide using the same speaker's notes you'll use for your actual presentation. Then click the Next button and continue for the next slide. As you continue to move through the slides of your presentation, PowerPoint will track your time.

NOTE *Aim for a delivery rate of 160 words a minute. This is the current average for business and technical presentations.*

After you complete your presentation, PowerPoint displays a Message box like the one shown in Figure 6-6. It shows the total time you spent for the slide show. You can also tell PowerPoint, simply by clicking the Yes button, that you want to record the time you spent on each slide and store this information with the slide. You might want to record your rehearsal timing information. You can later use these times to automate the display of the next slide, as discussed later in this step, in the section "Setting up for a delivery."

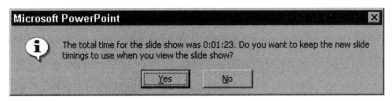

Figure 6-6   The Message box that PowerPoint uses to report rehearsal timing information.

NOTE   *Slide timing information appears in Slide Sorter view in the lower left corner of each slide.*

Voice and body language tips

To look and sound almost as professional as broadcasters and actors when you deliver your PowerPoint presentations, you can try several simple yet powerful techniques:

1. Speak in short phrases.

Get in the habit of speaking in short phrases rather than endless rambling sentences. A phrase is a group of words that express an idea. A phrase may not be a complete sentence. By short, we mean from 2 to 14 words, with the best lengths being about 5 to 9 words. Short phrases are easier to speak and easier to understand.

2. Pause after phrases.

Follow your short phrases with short pauses. Pauses allow time for ideas to sink in. As a proverb puts it, "When the words cease, the meaning flows on." Good speakers are not afraid to pause. A pause signals poise.

3. Drop pitch on endings.

To sound convincing and authoritative, end your phrases and sentences by dropping the pitch of your voice on the last syllable of the last word. If your pitch inflects up, you may sound wishy-washy, uncertain, as if you're seeking approval. Pitching down on endings communicates closure, completeness, and authority in American spoken English. It is the single most important thing you can do vocally to be a commanding speaker. Use this technique every time you introduce yourself, as actors and television broadcasters do.

Remember, drop the pitch (the musical note), not the volume. Let the last syllable be as loud as the first. Pitch down also at the end of most questions; the only questions we tend to raise our pitch on are questions that ask for a yes or no answer. Right?

TIP *Speaking in short phrases, followed by pauses, with a strong drop in pitch on endings can help you speak through extreme nervousness, as well as cure the "ahs" and "ums."*

4. Pitch up for emphasis.

To get your ideas across with impact, you must emphasize your key words vocally. To make ideas jump out, raise your pitch on the accented syllable of key words. For example, if you want to say, "We need more cooperation around here," cooperation would be your key idea. To make this idea stand out, emphasize the accented syllable in this word. You would still end the sentence by dropping your pitch.

5. Gesture naturally.

Let your hands move naturally as you speak to describe what you are saying. Gesture with both hands, shoulder-high (or higher for large crowds), with lively fingers (as if you're holding a beach ball in your hands). When you are not gesturing, your hands can hang loosely at your sides, or rest gently on a lectern. You can point at slides with your arms or use a laser pointer, as long as you don't wiggle the red dot excessively and create a visual distraction.

NOTE *If you hold an object to show the audience, please hold it still for five or six seconds so we can focus clearly on it; hold objects that you can handle easily right next to the left side of your face.*

6. Stand steady.

For a powerful stance, stand in one spot, with your feet planted shoulder-width apart, heels closer, toes fanned out slightly. Let your body sink into the earth (feel gravity acting), and let the earth's energy come up to animate your body. Generally, it's best to speak from one place, feet firmly on the floor, body animated from the ankles up. You can move to various spots as you talk, get set, and speak from there for a while. The point is: Avoid aimless wandering. Delivering information on the run, waters it down.

TIP *To look tall as a speaker, wear vertical, not horizontal lines; a man's tie should reach the belt buckle or lower. To look authoritative, wear dark-colored outer jackets (dark blue, dark gray; women can wear black), with light-colored shirts or blouses.*

Setting Up Your Presentation

After you've reviewed your presentation, created your speaker's notes, and rehearsed your presentation, you are ready to prepare for showing your presentation. This isn't difficult work, and it doesn't take long (especially after you've got some experience). But you often need to complete three basic tasks:

- Prepare the PowerPoint presentation file.

- Prepare whatever media you'll use for actually making the presentation. (This task may be very easy if you are going to simply show your presentation onscreen, but more difficult and time-consuming if you want to use 35mm slides or color transparencies.)

- Prepare any necessary handouts for your audience.

Preparing the presentation file

PowerPoint provides two commands you can use to prepare the presentation file for use in an actual presentation. PowerPoint's Custom Show command, which appears on the Slide Show menu, gives you an easy way to create a presentation by using only a subset of the presentation's slides. The Set Up Show command, which also appears on the Slide Show menu, provides some check boxes and option buttons you can use to fine-tune the way the presentation runs.

Creating a custom slide show

A *custom slide show* is just a list, or subset, of slides you want to display as a separate, customized presentation. To create a custom slide show, choose the Slide Show menu's Custom Shows command. PowerPoint displays the Custom Shows dialog box, as shown in Figure 6-7.

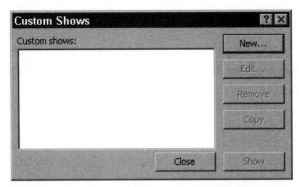

Figure 6-7   The Custom Shows dialog box.

When PowerPoint displays the Custom Shows dialog box, click the New button. PowerPoint then displays the Define Custom Show dialog box, as shown in Figure 6-8. This dialog box lists the slides that make up your presentation using the Slides In Presentation box.

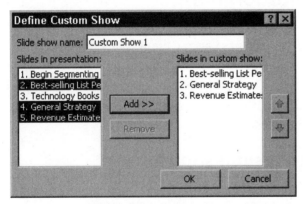

Figure 6-8   The Define Custom Show dialog box.

To create a custom presentation or a custom show using some subset of these slides, click the first slide you want to add to the custom show, and then click the Add button. PowerPoint adds the slide to the Slides In Custom Show list box. This shows you that the slide you just added is the first one in your custom show. To add slides, click them and then click the Add button. Add slides to the custom show in the same order you want them to appear. After you've defined or identified all the slides you want to appear, click the OK button.

NOTE   *You can move a slide shown in the Slides In Custom Show list box to a new position. To do this, click the slide to select it. Then click either the up-arrow or down-arrow button to the right of the Slides In Custom Show list box. When you do, PowerPoint moves the slide either up or down in the list.*

Setting up for a delivery

If you are going to use PowerPoint or the Pack And Go Wizard to deliver your presentation, you first want to set up the presentation. This process just ensures that your slides are fine-tuned for the way you'll show them.

NOTE   *The Pack And Go Wizard is discussed in the section "Using the Pack And Go Wizard."*

To set up your presentation's slides, choose the Slide Show menu's Set Up Show command. When you do, PowerPoint displays the Set Up Show dialog box, as shown in Figure 6-9.

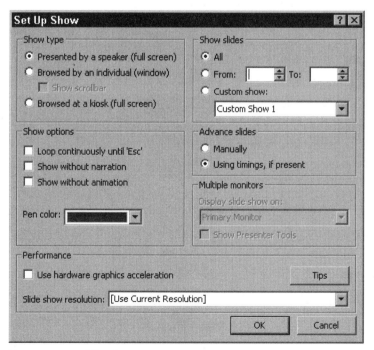

Figure 6-9   The Set Up Show dialog box.

You use this dialog box to fine-tune the presentation's slides and to specify how your presentation should progress from slide to slide. To use the dialog box, take the following steps:

1. Indicate how you'll deliver your presentation.

You mark the button in the Show Type area that corresponds to the way you will be presenting your presentation. If you will present the information in person, mark the Presented By A Speaker button. If you'll present the information by letting someone browse the slides of the presentation—in other words, you won't present the information; instead, audience members will view the information at their own pace—click the Browsed By An Individual button. If the information will be browsed at an unattended computer in a kiosk, click the Browsed At A Kiosk button.

NOTE   *The Show Scroll Bar check box provides another method for moving to the next slide. If you mark the Show Scrollbar check box, PowerPoint displays a scroll bar on the side of the Slide Show window. The Slide Show window that appears is available when you mark the Browsed By An Individual button. This scroll bar lets the individual browsing your presentation scroll through the presentation using the scroll bar.*

2. Indicate whether you want your slide show to loop.

If you want the presentation to continue, or loop continuously, mark the Loop Continuously Until 'Esc' box. If you mark this check box, PowerPoint continues to display the slides in the presentation one after another until someone presses the Escape key. This means that after the last slide in the presentation is presented, PowerPoint redisplays the first slide.

3. (Optional) Pick a pen color.

One other setup task you might want to complete is picking a pen color. PowerPoint lets you use a pen pointer if you want—you can draw on the slides using the mouse pointer during your presentation. You can use the Pen Color drop-down list box to pick the best color for your scribbling.

4. Indicate whether you want to use recorded narration.

If you don't want to include any narration you recorded for the presentation, leave the Show Without Narration box unchecked. If you do want to record any narration, check the box. (Typically, a business professional user of PowerPoint won't record narration for a PowerPoint presentation.)

NOTE   *To record narration for a presentation, you use the Slide Show menu's Record*
        Narration command.

5. **Indicate whether you want to use animation.**

If you want to show your presentation without animation, mark the Show Without Animation check box. If you do want to include any animation you set up on slides, unmark this check box, of course.

6. **Identify the slides that make up your presentation.**

Use the Show Slides area and its buttons to specify which slides should make up the presentation. For example, if you want to use all slides in the open presentation, mark the All button. Alternatively, if you want to show only some of the slides, mark the From button and then enter the first slide number you want in the From box and the last slide number you want in the To box. If you set up custom slide shows for a presentation, you can also mark the Custom Show button. When you mark this button, PowerPoint lets you select the custom show from the Custom Show drop-down list box.

7. **Tell PowerPoint when it should display the next slide.**

You can use the Advance Slides buttons—Manually and Using Timings If Present— to tell PowerPoint how or when it should display the next slide. If you're going to present the slide in person, you will probably click the Manually button. If you click the Manually button, PowerPoint expects someone to tell it that it should display the next slide. You tell PowerPoint that you want to display the next slide by pressing the space bar or clicking the slide with the mouse. If you're not going to display or deliver a presentation in person, perhaps the slide show will be viewed at a computer in a kiosk, for example, mark the Using Timings If Present button. This tells PowerPoint that it should use the rehearsal timings you will have created as part of rehearsing for your presentation.

8. **(Optional) Tell PowerPoint which monitor to use.**

If you use multiple monitors on your computer, you can use the Display Slide Show On the box to select the monitor PowerPoint uses to display the slide show.

9. **(Optional) Tell PowerPoint to boost your computer's performance.**

The Performance area of the Set Up Show dialog box includes boxes you can use to boost the slide show speed. You may be able to boost the slide show speed by checking the Use Hardware Graphics Acceleration box. You may also want to boost the slide show speed by seleting a lower screen resolution from the Slide Show Resolution box.

Preparing any necessary presentation media

How you will package your presentation and the media you use depends on the technology you've selected. You have roughly three choices available:

- Display the slides of your presentation either on your own computer or by using the color projector that projects your computer's screen onto a larger surface.

- Use 35mm slides.

- Use color transparencies and an overhead transparency projector.

NOTE   *Obviously, if you are going to use a 35mm slide media, you'll need a 35mm slide projector. If you are going to use color transparencies, you'll also need an overhead transparency projector.*

NOTE   *For information on publishing a presentation to a web server, refer to the section "Delivering Your Presentation Via the Web" in "Step 7: Deliver Your Presentation." You can probably also consult your firm's web administrator.*

Showing your presentation on your computer

If you are presenting your slides to a small group, you might be able to do this right from your laptop. For example, if you are making a presentation to a small group around a conference table, it might be that your laptop, especially if it has a color monitor, works fine for sharing your slides.

If you are going to go this route, you don't need to do anything special to prepare your presentation. All you need to remember is this: to start your presentation, simply choose the View menu's Slide Show command.

Using a color projector

Using a color projector should be no more complicated than using your own computer's monitor or screen. In fact, all you often need to do is plug in the projector's cable into the video socket on the back of your laptop. Your laptop computer probably includes a video output socket such as the one you might use to plug in a full-size monitor. This same socket is usually the one you use to plug in a color projector. Note, then, that a color projector—from the perspective of your laptop—works just like another big monitor.

Using color transparencies

Many printers, and especially many color printers, will print on blank transparencies. Therefore you might be able to use color transparencies for your presentation.

If you are going to use color transparencies, you typically take the following steps:

1. Tell PowerPoint that you want to produce overhead slides.

PowerPoint needs to size the slides used for overhead transparencies slightly differently from the way it sizes slides for other types of presentations. To tell PowerPoint that you want your slides sized for overhead transparencies, choose the File menu's Page Setup command. When PowerPoint displays the Page Setup dialog box, as shown in Figure 6-10, select the Overhead size from the Slides Sized For list box.

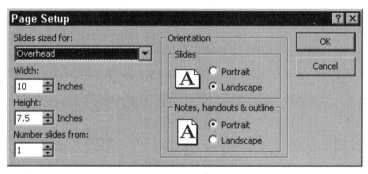

Figure 6-10 The Page Setup dialog box.

2. Print the transparencies.

After you've told PowerPoint that you want to produce overhead transparencies, you can print the transparencies, assuming that you have a color printer. To do this, choose the File menu's Print command. Use the Print dialog box, as shown in Figure 6-11, to specify that you want to print slides. To do this, select the Slides entry from the Print What drop-down list box. If you are going to print overhead transparencies on a color printer, verify that the Color/Grayscale box shows Color. After you've done this, click the OK button to print the slides.

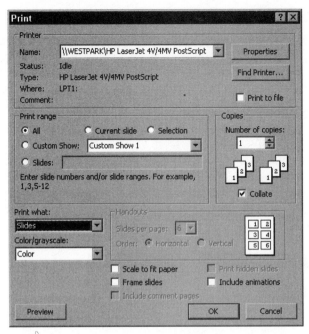

Figure 6-11 The Print dialog box.

NOTE *If you don't have a color printer or you don't want to print in color, you can also print black or grayscale versions of your slides and use them as transparencies. Obviously, your transparencies in this case are going to be in black, gray, and white. To print overhead transparencies in black-and-white, select Pure Black And White from the Color/Grayscale box. To print overhead transparencies in black, gray, and white, select Grayscale from the Color/Grayscale box.*

Using 35mm slides

You can produce 35mm slides for individual slides that make up your PowerPoint presentation. How you do this depends on what sort of equipment you have or don't have in-house.

If you have a film recorder attached to your network or desktop computer, you can print your PowerPoint slides directly to the film recorder. The film recorder will then create 35mm slides based on the PowerPoint slides. You'll then need to take this undeveloped film to a film processor that will develop 35mm slides you can use in your presentation.

To print slides to a film recorder, take the following steps:

1. **Size your slides.**

   To size your slides so that they're appropriate for 35mm slides, choose the File menu's Page Setup command. When PowerPoint displays the Page Setup dialog box, as shown in Figure 6-12, choose the 35mm Slides entry from the Slides Sized For drop-down list box. Then click OK.

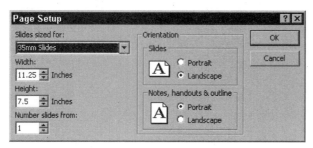

Figure 6-12 The Page Setup dialog box.

2. **Print the slides to your film recorder.**

   After you've sized the slides so that they work on 35mm slides, choose the File menu's Print command. When PowerPoint displays the Print dialog box, choose the Film Recorder entry from the Name drop-down list box. In other words, you print to the Film Recorder. After you do this, verify that the Print What drop-down list box indicates that you're printing slides, and verify that the Color/Grayscale box shows Color—if you are printing to 35mm slides, you want to use color.

   After you've specified how PowerPoint should print, click the OK button. PowerPoint prints the slides to the film recorder. All you'll need to do next is have the film developed.

To create 35mm slides when you don't have a film recorder—most people probably don't—you need to send the PowerPoint presentation to a service bureau that will convert your PowerPoint slides to 35mm slides. As you might guess, this just means that the service bureau has a computer attached to a film recorder. You might be able to look up such a service bureau in your local business or telephone directory. You can also use the Genigraphics Service Bureau.

NOTE *To use the Genigraphics Service Bureau, visit the Genigraphics web site at www.genigraphics.com and click the Order Online hyperlink. This starts an online wizard that steps you through process of ordering presentation materials.*

NOTE *You can also call Genigraphics directly for information on how to work through the mail. The Genigraphics telephone number is 1-800-790-4001.*

Preparing any handouts

One final task you probably want to do is prepare any handouts. Handouts commonly include black-and-white copies of the screens or slides you'll show. If you hand these out as part of your presentation, your audience might be able to take notes. Or, alternatively, you might choose to hand out handouts *after* your presentation, as a way to remind the audience about what you said.

In either case, producing handouts is straightforward. To produce handouts that show your PowerPoint slides, take the following steps:

1. **Tell PowerPoint you want to print slide information.**

    To tell PowerPoint that you want to print slide information, choose the File menu's Print command. When you do, PowerPoint displays the Print dialog box, as shown in Figure 6-13.

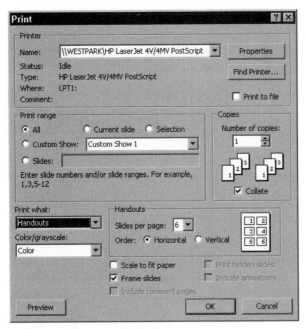

Figure 6-13 The Print dialog box.

2. **Tell PowerPoint that you want to create handouts.**

   To tell PowerPoint that you want to create handouts, select Handouts from the Print What drop-down list box. You should also use the check boxes at the bottom of the Print dialog box to indicate whether you are printing in grayscale or pure black-and-white.

3. **Describe the handouts.**

   Use the Handouts area and its boxes and buttons to describe how you want PowerPoint to print the handouts. Use the Slides Per Page drop-down list box, for example, to tell PowerPoint how many slides it should print on each page. Use the Order buttons to indicate how PowerPoint should arrange slide images on each page.

   After you've described the handouts you want, click the OK button. PowerPoint then prints the handouts in the way you specified.

NOTE *If you print three slides per page, PowerPoint includes lines that audience members can use to jot down notes about the slides.*

NOTE *Use the Number Of Copies box if you want to print multiple copies of your handouts; otherwise, you'll need to use a photocopy machine.*

Using the Pack And Go Wizard

You don't actually need the PowerPoint program in order to show a presentation. You can create a stand-alone version of a presentation that includes all the slides in your presentation and a PowerPoint browser program, which lets you show those slides.

To create such a stand-alone presentation, you first need to create the presentation and then prepare it so that it is set up just the way you want it, as described in the preceding paragraphs. After you've done this, you can use the Pack And Go Wizard to create your stand-alone presentation. To do this, choose the File menu's Pack And Go command. PowerPoint starts the Pack And Go Wizard. Figure 6-14 shows the first dialog box that the Pack And Go Wizard displays. To use the wizard, just answer its questions by clicking buttons and filling in boxes.

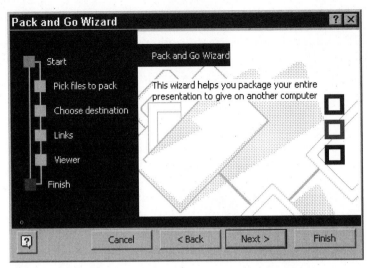

Figure 6-14 The first Pack And Go Wizard dialog box.

The Pack And Go Wizard assumes that you want to package the open presentation, as the wizard's dialog box shown in Figure 6-15 indicates. But you can package any presentation you've already created.

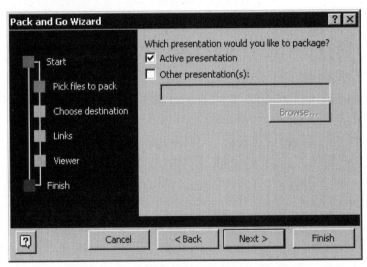

Figure 6-15 The second Pack And Go Wizard dialog box.

The Pack And Go Wizard asks which removable disk you want to use to create the stand-alone presentation using the dialog box shown in Figure 6-16. The wizard's other dialog boxes ask you about which building blocks, such as linked files and fonts, you want to bundle with your presentation. (Your best bet is to simply accept the default or suggested settings if you have questions.)

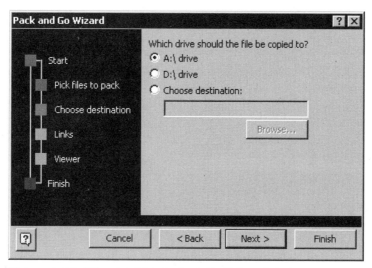

Figure 6-16 The third Pack And Go Wizard dialog box.

After you've provided this information, you simply click Finish. PowerPoint then creates a stand-alone version of your presentation and copies this information to the removable disk you've indicated. PowerPoint will also copy the PowerPoint Viewer program you use to view this stand-alone program.

NOTE   *The PowerPoint Viewer program, when it is installed, takes roughly 5 megabytes of disk space.*

NOTE   *How you use the PowerPoint Viewer program is described in "Step 7: Deliver Your Presentation."*

Step 7

DELIVER YOUR PRESENTATION

Featuring:

- Starting and Ending Your Presentation
- Delivering a Presentation in Person
- Delivering an Individually Controlled PowerPoint Presentation
- Using a Kiosk
- Delivering Your Presentation Via the Web
- Online Meetings and Presentation Broadcasting

Even after you create your presentation, you have some final decisions to make. (PowerPoint provides almost half a dozen different ways you can present your slides.) What is more, if you're the person presenting, there are tactics you can employ to add to value and impact of your presentation in the pages that follow, we discuss these topics.

Starting and Ending Your Presentation

When you present in person, you encounter the added challenge of standing in front of your audience and guiding them through your slides. As with many tasks, practice and experience make this work much easier and smoother. Even new presenters, however, can improve their performance by taking the following five steps as they start:

1. **Greet your audience by smiling.**

    Let your first words greet the audience graciously, with lively energy. Say not, "good morning," but "GOOD MORNING!" Roger Ailes wrote, "An ounce of energy is worth a pound of technique." Wear a friendly face and a genuine smile. As you speak words, look into the eyes of one person in the audience for one or two seconds, then another person, and another. Smile at least at the beginning and end of each presentation: Let a smile be the bookends of your talk.

    NOTE *As you greet the audience, you may want to display your first PowerPoint slide that states the title of your presentation. The slide might include title, name of organization, name of presenter, logo, and a graphic element.*

2. **State a question.**

    After greeting the audience, ask a question. Questions often create a quest because they grab and then focus the minds of listeners, pulling them into your topic. You can experiment with four kinds of questions:

    *   Direct questions, such as "How many of you have ever received great customer service?" People often raise their hands, giving you information about them.

    *   Framed questions, such as "The question before us today is: How can we give outstanding customer service that people will never forget?"

    *   Story questions, such as "Imagine this…" then tell a brief story, or give a set of facts, and follow with a direct or framed question.

    *   Multiple-choice questions, such as "When customers come to us with a complaint, what do you think they want most: To be heard with empathy, to have the problem fixed, or to have it made up to them?" Multiple-choice questions are popular on TV quiz shows.

    NOTE *You can put your question on a slide. Framed questions work especially well on slides.*

3. **Make a promise.**

    After opening your presentation with a greeting and a question, follow with a promise. Your promise line does two things: It previews what you'll give ("Today, I will…"), and promises what they'll gain ("so that you will…"). "Today (this morning, next 20 minutes), I will (explain, present, give, show, teach, explore, share) three (use a number instead of "some") easy ways to handle customer complaints so that you will understand what customers really want, and you'll be able to send customers away satisfied and smiling (include at least two benefits or rewards the listeners will gain from your talk)."

4. State your name and credentials.

Now introduce yourself by saying your name—if your audience doesn't already know it—and then establish credibility by briefly explaining why you are qualified to talk about this topic. You might choose to share your job title, company or organization, years of experience, or something you have in common with the audience that allows them to bond with you. Even if you have been introduced, you may still want to share something about yourself that was not said to add credibility or heighten anticipation.

NOTE   *It's not common to use a slide for describing your credentials, although you might choose to do so. More commonly, presenters provide this information verbally.*

5. Invite questions during or later.

Let listeners know when you want their participation with one of two signals: "If you have questions or comments as I speak, please raise your hand." Or, "After my presentation, I'll be happy to take your questions and comments."

When you reach the end of your presentation, you should signal the end is near with lines such as, "Finally," "In conclusion," or "In summary." This is the time the audience reawakens. It's the time to do one of two things, or both.

1. Summarize.

You can use a slide to list key points that you've covered, of course, as we discuss in "Step 2: Outline Your Content." But you may also have other points—perhaps those raised by the audience in their questions—that you want to summarize, too.

2. Call to action.

If the purpose of your presentation was to persuade listeners to take some action, be sure to make this request. In fact, you should have a slide that supports or explicitly makes this request. In making the request, you can use three degrees of "push": *invite* them to take the action; *encourage* them; or *challenge* them to act.

Do everything in your power to end all presentations on a note of positive hope. As Samuel Johnson reminded us, in our minds we live "not from pleasure to pleasure, but from hope to hope." Give listeners something to hope for as you conclude, especially if the presentation contained bad news.

A simple clear way to end presentations is with these four words: "Thank you for listening." If you want questions, don't whimper, "Any questions"? Instead, open your arms and invite the audience this way: "And now I welcome your questions and comments." And wait for several seconds for the first courageous person to speak.

Delivering a Presentation in Person

You can deliver your presentation in person, the most common method that is used. When you deliver your presentation in person, you probably use the PowerPoint program itself to show the slides. You aren't required to use the PowerPoint program though. You can also use the PowerPoint Viewer. Both techniques are described in the sections that follow.

Running the slide show using PowerPoint

If you're showing your presentation on a laptop computer, simply choose the Slide Show menu's View Show command. When you do this, PowerPoint displays the first slide in your presentation.

If you've indicated that you want to move manually from slide to slide, press the space bar or use the mouse to click on the slide when you want to move to the next slide.

If you've indicated that you want to use rehearsal timings to move from slide to slide, simply wait for the rehearsal time to pass.

At the end of your slide presentation, PowerPoint displays a blank or black screen. You might want to leave this screen displayed because it is a good way to end your presentation. You can also move beyond this blank, black screen to the PowerPoint program window or the PowerPoint Viewer window.

TIP   *If you're using a color projector, verify that the slides are readable—people sitting in the last row should be able to read the smallest word or number. To do this, fill the entire screen with your projected slide. Often, you need to move the projector back farther from the screen until the image goes close to the edges. Also, try to project images on the upper portion of the screen rather than on the lower so that no one's head blocks the view. Remember: The bigger the visual aid, the bigger the impact.*

If you've told PowerPoint that the slide show should loop continuously, remember that you need to press the Escape key to terminate the slide show. You can also right-click the slide so that PowerPoint displays the Shortcuts menu. When the Shortcuts menu is displayed, choose the End Show command to stop the slide show.

Reviewing the slide Shortcuts menu commands

If you right-click a slide during a presentation, PowerPoint displays a Shortcuts menu of commands you might find useful during the presentation. Figure 7-1 shows the Shortcuts menu.

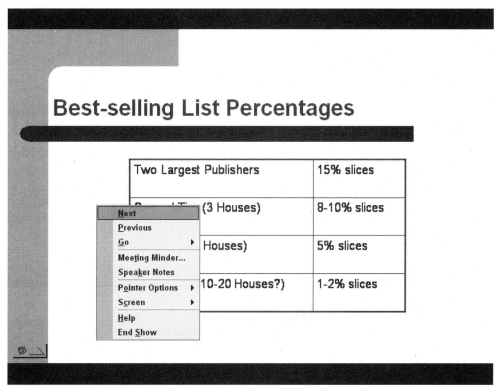

Figure 7-1   The Shortcuts menu.

The first two commands, Next and Previous, do what you expect. If you choose the Next command, PowerPoint displays the next slide or animation effect in the presentation. If you choose the Previous command, PowerPoint displays the previous slide or animation effect in the presentation.

You can also use the Go command to display a submenu that lets you choose specific slides. To use the Slide Navigator to choose a slide, choose the Slide Navigator command from the Go submenu. Then when PowerPoint displays the Slide Navigator dialog box, shown in Figure 7-2, double-click the slide you want to view. To choose a specific slide, choose the By Title command from the Go submenu. Then when PowerPoint displays the sub-submenu, choose the slide you want to see.

To display the slides in a custom slide show, choose the Custom Show command from the Go submenu. Then when PowerPoint displays a menu of the custom slide shows you've created, click the custom slide show you want. To display the last slide you displayed choose the Previously Viewed command from the Go submenu.

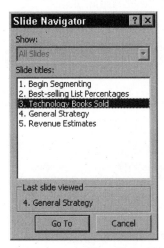

Figure 7-2   The Slide Navigator dialog box.

The Shortcuts menu also displays two commands that let you, in effect, jump outside the presentation. The Meeting Minder command displays the Meeting Minder dialog box, as shown in Figure 7-3. The Meeting Minder dialog box lets you keep minutes or notes of a presentation meeting.

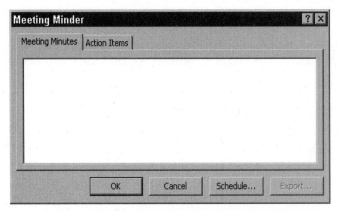

Figure 7-3   The Meeting Minutes tab of the Meeting Minder dialog box.

You can also use its Action Items tab, shown in Figure 7-4, to record action items or to-do list items that stem from the presentation and meeting.

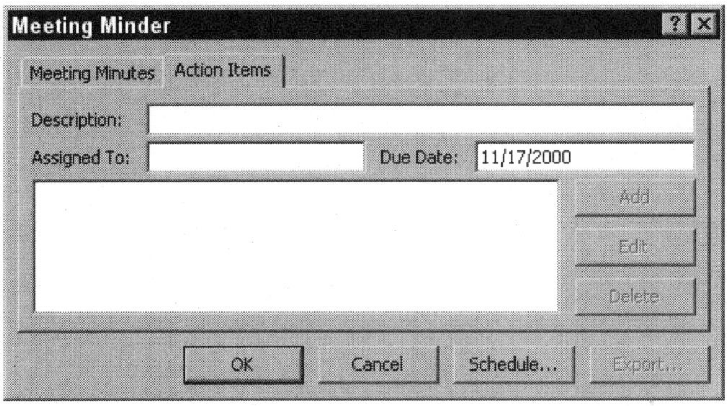

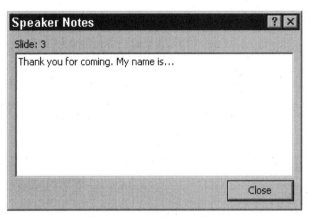

Figure 7-4   The Action Items tab of the Meeting Minder dialog box.

The Speaker Notes command displays a Speaker Notes dialog box, as shown in Figure 7-5. This box shows the speaker's notes for the slide that's displayed. If you forget your speaker's notes or want to review or share them publicly, you can choose this command.

Speaker Notes

Slide: 3

Thank you for coming. My name is...

Close

Figure 7-5   The Speaker Notes dialog box.

The Pointer Options command on the Shortcuts menu displays a submenu of commands you can use to control what the mouse pointer looks like and what it does. What you will typically want to do with this menu is either choose the Hidden command to remove the mouse pointer from the screen or choose the Pen command to turn the mouse into a pen. If you turn the mouse pointer into a pen, you can drag the mouse pointer to mark the slide with temporary drawn lines. You can use this "pen" to underline, circle, or diagram on the slide, as shown in Figure 7-6.

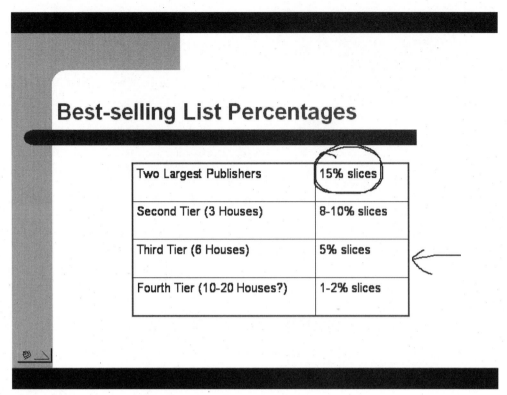

Figure 7-6   A slide with pen markings on it.

NOTE   *If you choose to use the mouse pen pointer, you might want to use the Pen Color command, which also appears on the Pointer Options submenu. If you choose the Pen Color command, PowerPoint displays a menu that lists colors you can use for the pen. Pick a pen color that gives maximum contrast with the slide background and the colors used for the slide objects. In this way, your pen markings will be most legible.*

The Help command, which also appears on the Shortcuts menu, is worth mentioning. Figure 7-7 shows the dialog box that appears when you choose this command. This Slide Show Help dialog box provides a quick list of keys you can press to accomplish certain actions while showing your presentation. For example, reading from the top of the Slide Show Help dialog box, you can see that left-clicking, pressing the space bar, pressing the letter *N*, pressing the down-arrow or right-arrow key, or pressing Enter all tell PowerPoint to advance to the next slide. Review the ways you can navigate through the slides in a show to discover the method that works best for you.

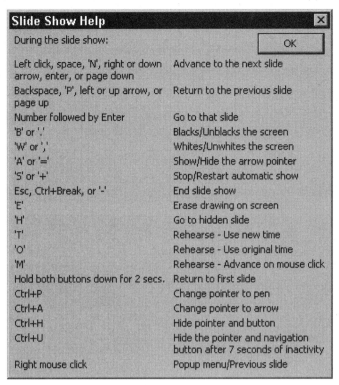

Figure 7-7 The Slide Show Help dialog box.

We won't repeat the other information shown in this dialog box, but remember that this help information is easily available to you.

NOTE   *The term* slide show *used in Figure 7-7 might not make much sense if you've been reading this book since page 1, because we've avoided the term and instead used the term* presentation. *You can, however, distinguish between the two terms. A* slide show *consists of slides you'll show to your audience, including possibly all the slides in your presentation. However, if you have hidden slides or have created a custom slide show or have just decided to display only a contiguous range of slides in your presentation, there might be slides in your presentation that aren't in your slide show. A* presentation, *as we discussed in "Step 1: Learn the Logic," is the complete set of slides you've created.*

Running a slide show using the PowerPoint Viewer

If you created a stand-alone presentation using the Pack And Go Wizard, you'll need to set up the PowerPoint Viewer program and then start it in order to deliver your presentation.

NOTE: *The Pack And Go Wizard is described in "Step 6: Prepare Your Presentation."*

Setting up the PowerPoint Viewer

To set up the PowerPoint Viewer program, first find or create an empty folder. Then open the setup program on the disk you created using the Pack And Go Wizard. You can do this by viewing the disk and using a tool like Windows Explorer or the My Computer window. When you view the disk you created with the Pack And Go Wizard, you'll see the setup program, as shown in Figure 7-8. To start the setup program, double-click its icon.

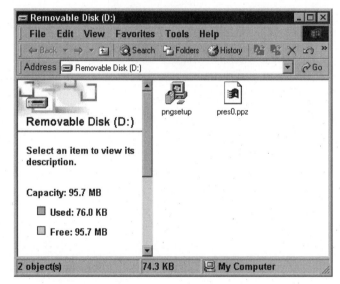

Figure 7-8   The My Computer window showing a disk created with the Pack And Go Wizard.

The setup program asks you for the folder in which the PowerPoint Viewer should be installed, as shown in Figure 7-9. After the PowerPoint Viewer is installed, the setup program asks whether you want to run the slide show. Click the Yes button.

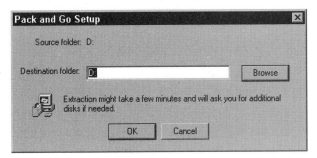

Figure 7-9 The Pack And Go Setup dialog box.

Using the PowerPoint Viewer

To start the PowerPoint Viewer, use a program like Windows Explorer to see the contents of the folder you used for the installation. Then double-click the PowerPoint Viewer item.

NOTE *When you install the PowerPoint Viewer, you have the option of starting the slide show.*

The Microsoft PowerPoint Viewer dialog box, lists the contents of the PowerPoint Presentations folder. You will probably see only one—the one you set up using the Pack And Go Wizard. To view this presentation using the Viewer, click the presentation to select it and then click the Show button. When you do, PowerPoint displays the first slide in the presentation. To move to the next slide, press the space bar or click the mouse.

NOTE *You can download a free copy of the PowerPoint Viewer program from the Microsoft web site:* http://www.officeupdate.microsoft.com/welcome powerpoint.asp.

The PowerPoint Viewer dialog box also includes the Print and Option buttons. The Print button prints slides from the selected presentation.

The Options button displays the Options dialog box which lets you change some of the presentation specifications you would have set up previously.

If the Password Locked Slide Show check box is checked in the Microsoft PowerPoint Viewer dialog box, PowerPoint asks for a *kiosk password* as you start the presentation using the PowerPoint Viewer. PowerPoint asks you to enter a password and then confirm the password you've entered, starts the presentation, and then runs the slide show according to your specifications. However, it won't stop the slide show for anyone who can't enter the password. In other words, if you or somebody else attempts to stop the slide show by pressing the Escape key, the PowerPoint Viewer asks for a password. If the person requesting that the slide show be stopped can supply the password, the PowerPoint Viewer will stop the slide show. If someone can't supply the password, however, the PowerPoint Viewer won't stop.

Delivering an Individually Controlled PowerPoint Presentation

If you have indicated, as part of setting up your slide show, that an individual will control the show, choose the View menu's Slide Show command. When you do, PowerPoint displays your slide show using a web browser like the one shown in Figure 7-10. This web browser works the same as other web browsers. For example, to move from one slide to another, you simply click the Back or Forward buttons.

NOTE   *You indicate an individual will control the slide show by choosing the Slide Show menu's Set Up Show command and by then, when PowerPoint displays the Set Up Show dialog box, marking the Browsed By An Individual button. For more information about the Set Up Show command refer to "Step 6: Prepare Your Presentation"*

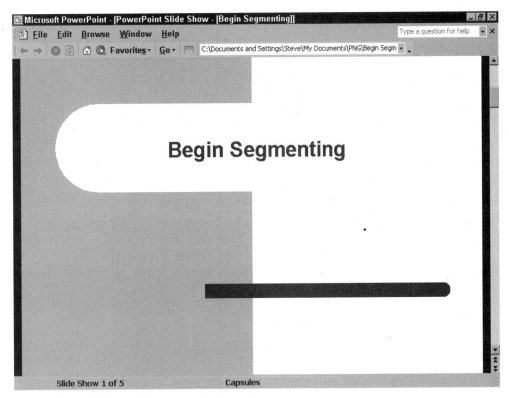

Figure 7-10 The web browser window.

NOTE *If you have set up the presentation to use rehearsal timings, you don't even need to click the Back or Forward buttons. PowerPoint will automatically advance to the next slide when the rehearsal timing time has passed.*

To stop an individually controlled slide show, press the Escape key. When you do this, PowerPoint redisplays the PowerPoint program window.

Using a Kiosk

If you set up the slide show to be delivered using an unattended computer in a kiosk, choose the View menu's Slide Show command. PowerPoint then displays the slide that's first in your presentation. Based on rehearsal timings, PowerPoint automatically moves from slide to slide.

If you check the Loop Continuously Until 'Esc' box, PowerPoint repeats the presentation. When PowerPoint displays the last slide in the slide show, it restarts the presentation and redisplays the first slide in the slide show.

Delivering Your Presentation Via the Web

If you have a web server, you can publish a PowerPoint presentation to a web site. After you do this, anyone with the ability to view that web site can view the slides in your presentation. After the presentation has been published to the web site, the PowerPoint slides become, in essence, web pages.

Creating PowerPoint web pages

To publish a PowerPoint presentation to a web site, take the following steps:

1. **Open the presentation.**

   Open the presentation you want to publish. If you have more than one presentation open, verify that the presentation you want to publish is the active presentation.

2. **Tell PowerPoint that you want to publish the presentation to the Web.**

   To tell PowerPoint that you want to publish the presentation to the Web, choose the File menu's Save As Web Page command. When you do, PowerPoint displays the Save As dialog box, as shown in Figure 7-11.

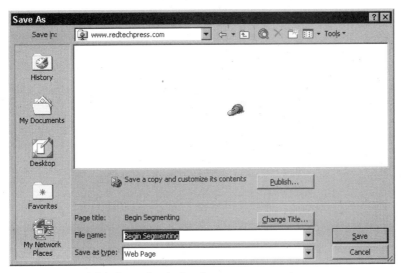

Figure 7-11 The Save As dialog box.

3. Describe how PowerPoint should create the web pages.

With the Save As dialog box displayed, click the Publish button. When you do, PowerPoint displays the Publish As Web Page dialog box, as shown in Figure 7-12.

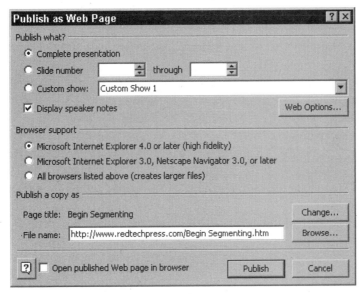

Figure 7-12 The Publish As Web Page dialog box.

Use the Publish What? buttons to indicate whether you want to publish the complete presentation or just a range of slides. Use the Browser Support buttons to indicate for which web browser you want to publish the presentation.

To describe what you want to publish and the browser you want to support, use the Publish A Copy As area to specify where you want to publish the presentation.

You can enter in the File Name box the pathname you want to use. The full pathname includes the drive letter, the folder name, any subfolder names, and the filename. If you don't know the pathname, click the Browse button to display the Publish As dialog box. This dialog box lets you work with the familiar Save In box and Save In list box to identify the location you want to use for the web pages.

4. Publish the web pages.

After you describe where you want to publish the web pages, click the Publish button. PowerPoint then creates an HTML, or web page, version of your presentation and saves it in the specified location.

Viewing PowerPoint web pages

To view the web version of the PowerPoint presentation, simply open the web page, or HTML document, that PowerPoint creates. Figure 7-13 shows how a PowerPoint presentation looks after it has been published as a web page. In the frame along the left edge of the web browser window, PowerPoint displays a list of the slides in the presentation. This list is actually a list of hyperlinks. You can click a slide to display the slide in the main portion of the web browser window. In a small frame below the actual slide frame, the Browser window will also show your speaker's notes.

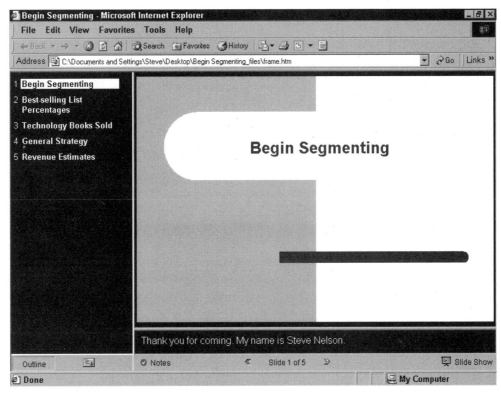

Figure 7-13 A PowerPoint web page.

If you publish the PowerPoint web page to a web server that's connected to the Internet, you will be able to view the PowerPoint presentation from any other computer that's connected to the Internet. This means, of course, that another option you have for delivering your presentation is by having people view the web pages with their web browsers.

Online Meetings and Presentation Broadcasting

PowerPoint includes two advanced delivery technologies: online meetings and presentation broadcasting. An *online meeting* lets you show a PowerPoint presentation on multiple computers, if all the computers are connected to a network. An online meeting also provides a white board you can use to collect comments from the meeting participants.

A *presentation broadcast* lets you deliver a presentation over a network. PowerPoint comes with the tools and software you need to deliver a presentation broadcast of as many as 15 people over a network. But Microsoft sells another product, Net Show Server, which runs on a Windows 2000 server and lets you show presentation broadcasts to much larger groups of people.

Some business professionals might want to explore the online meeting and presentation broadcasting tools. However, in our opinion, these tools require significantly more PowerPoint and Microsoft Windows expertise than the typical executive user already possesses or wants to acquire. For that reason, these two PowerPoint delivery tools aren't discussed here. If you want information about how to use them, refer to the *PowerPoint User's Guide or PowerPoint's online help.*

Appendix A

CREATING BETTER CHARTS WITH MICROSOFT GRAPH

Featuring:

- Fundamentals of Good Chart Design
- Strengths and Limits of Various Chart Types
- Avoiding Common Charting Mistakes

Although Microsoft Graph makes it very easy to create a chart that looks good, you'll find creating truly useful graphics more difficult. For this reason, it seems fair to spend just a few minutes discussing some of the ideas that the people who think about such things have in regard to creating good charts.

NOTE   *If you get interested in the subject of using charts to convey quantitative information, consider looking at one of Edward Tufte's books. His books on using charts and other graphics images to display quantitative information are arguably the very best books on these subjects—and fun to read.*

Fundamentals of Good Chart Design

Let's start this discussion by pointing out that when you create a chart, you do so to let the chart viewer compare data. This seemingly trivial observation usually produces some valuable insights into good chart design. It turns out that there are really only five types of data comparisons you or anyone else can make. These data comparisons largely determine which type of chart you should use.

To add concreteness to this discussion, let's say that your organization has some reason for researching religious affiliation in the United States. With a complete and rich data set, you could make any of these five data comparisons:

- Part-to-whole comparisons.

  In a part-to-whole comparison, you show how the pieces make up a whole. For example, in a graph showing religious affiliation information, the whole might be the entire U.S. population. The pieces might be the number of people affiliated with particular religious groups, faiths, sects, and denominations, such as Anglicans, Baptists, and Catholics. In a part-to-whole comparison, then, you might compare the number of Anglicans to the entire U.S. population, the number of Baptists to the entire U.S. population, and so on.

- Whole-to-whole comparisons.

  In a whole-to-whole comparison, you compare whole items to each other. You use whole-to-whole comparisons to compare absolute numbers. For example, if you were again preparing a chart that shows religious affiliation, you could compare the absolute number of Anglicans to the absolute number of Baptists and to the absolute number of Catholics. You might also compare the absolute number of atheists to the absolute number of agnostics, for example. All these comparisons are whole-to-whole comparisons.

- Time-series comparisons.

  In a time-series comparison, you show how some variable or value changes over time. If you want to show the growth, decline, or steady state of Catholics in the United States, you would use a time-series chart.

- Correlation comparisons.

  A correlation comparison shows how two variables are related or not related. For example, if you wanted to use a graph that shows how attendance or affiliation with churches, synagogues, and mosques varies with the changes in the national income (assume that they do), you might be able to do so using a correlation comparison.

- Data-map comparisons.

  In a data-map comparison, you show how some variable changes geographically. You might use a data-map comparison to show how religious affiliation varies geographically. You could use such a data-map comparison to see, for example, whether the largest population of Southern Baptists really does live in the southern United States.

NOTE   *The Microsoft Graph application that you have available from PowerPoint lets you create charts that make the first four types of data comparisons listed in this section. You can't create the fifth, the data-map comparison, however, using Microsoft Graph. Note, though, that Microsoft Office includes another program, Map Point, that does allow you to create a data-map comparison. You could use one of these data-map comparisons created by Map Point on a PowerPoint slide. For more information about how to use an object created by one application or program in PowerPoint, refer to the discussion in "Step 3: Add Objects."*

After you understand that you can make five basic types of data comparisons using a chart, picking a chart type becomes quite straightforward. Different chart types make different comparisons. Therefore, by identifying the data comparison you need to make, you often implicitly pick a chart type and always narrow the list of appropriate charts you should choose from.

- To make a part-to-whole data comparison, you need to use a pie chart. No other chart makes this data comparison.

- To make a whole-to-whole data comparison, you need to use a bar chart, column chart, radar chart, or surface chart. Note that some of these types of charts can be displayed in either two-dimensional or three-dimensional format.

- To make a time-series data comparison, you need to use a chart that uses a *horizontal* data category axis—the horizontal axis shows the passage of time. So, you could use area charts, column charts, combination charts, and line charts for time-series data comparisons. Again, some of these types of charts can be shown in either a two-dimensional or three-dimensional format.

- To show a correlation comparison, you can use only an XY chart, also sometimes called a scatter chart.

- Finally, as noted earlier, you can't make a data-map comparison using Microsoft Graph. You need to use a data-mapping program to create a data map object and then copy this data map object to the PowerPoint slide.

NOTE   *If you're not familiar with the terms* data value, data series, *and* data category, *you might want to refer to the discussion "Using Charts" in "Step 3: Add Objects." It defines these three key charting terms.*

Strengths and Limits of Various Chart Types

This discussion doesn't need to take a lot of time, but we want to quickly discuss some of the commonly ascribed strengths and limits of the different chart types you will have available as you work with Microsoft Graph. Because we discuss or introduce an alleged strength or limit here doesn't mean that you should or shouldn't use a chart. Nonetheless, you might want to reflect on these discussions as you choose your own chart types. Even if you don't hold the thoughts shared here, some members of your audience might.

Area charts' strengths and limits

Area charts, like the one shown in Figure A-1, possess several noteworthy strengths. First, they let you plot very large numbers of data values. Individual data values simply appear as points along the line—meaning you can create an area chart that shows hundreds of data values. Area charts work well for showing trends in the first data series and in the total of all the data series.

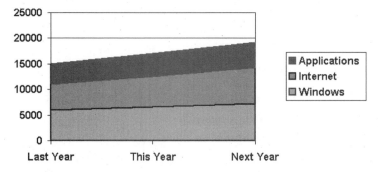

Figure A-1 An area chart.

One thing to note is that you can't really use an area chart for showing a trend in the second and any subsequent data series. An area chart stacks the data series values—that's how it creates the colored areas shown on the chart. This means that it becomes impossible to really compare trends in the subsequent data series.

One other unique strength of an area chart is that you can often create an implicit data series and, if the stacked lines equal some meaningful value, the stacked lines amount to another data series. For example, if you have a data series for expenses and profits and the sum of expenses and profits is revenue, you can create an area chart that plots expense data and profit data. The total area shown by these two data series equals a third, implicit data series: revenues.

Despite the strengths that area charts offer, they also possess several limits. You can't compare individual data points or data values. You probably won't be able to identify or guess at individual data values. And area charts might suggest trends that don't really exist or might not be meaningful (particularly if you use an axis that is scaled incorrectly or unintelligently).

Bar charts' strengths and limits

Bar charts are very useful for making whole-to-whole comparisons, particularly when the categories are *not* time intervals. The reason that this type works so well is that each data point is shown by an individual data marker, or bar. And as long as you don't use three-dimensional bars, it's relatively easy to precisely compare one bar to another bar by using an appropriately calibrated values axis. Figure A-2 shows a bar chart.

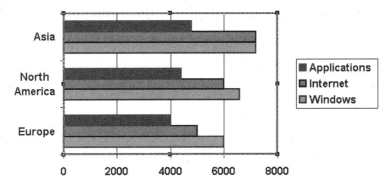

Figure A-2   A bar chart.

Two limits are associated with bar charts. Because each individual data value is depicted on its own bar, you can't ever work with very large data sets using a bar chart, particularly when you are talking about a bar chart you want to use on a PowerPoint slide. As you add bars to a bar chart, bar widths narrow, and, as the bar width narrows, the chart becomes less legible.

Another limit related to bar charts concerns a bar chart subtype called a *stacked* bar chart. This type of chart stacks the bars within a data category. Although a stacked bar chart can sometimes be useful, it doesn't really let you make good whole-to-whole comparisons. You can compare the first data series values using a stacked bar chart, but you can't compare subsequent data series.

Column charts' strengths and limits

Column charts work well for making time-series data comparisons when you are not working with a lengthy time horizon. To show how some data value, such as revenues or profits, changes over a few years, for example, a column chart works very well. The horizontal category axis depicts the passage of time in a conventional format (at least for European and American chart viewers), and the individual data markers, or the columns, precisely indicate the underlined data values. Figure A-3 shows a column chart.

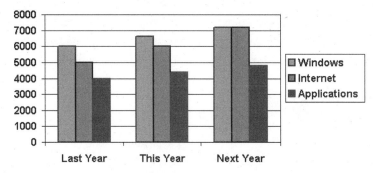

Figure A-3   A column chart.

Column charts suffer from several limits. Like their cousin the bar chart, column charts don't let you plot a large number of data values. The more data values, series, or categories you plot, the narrower and less legible the columns become. Another problem with column charts is that because category labels go under the horizontal axis, you often don't have much room for good, descriptive category labels. You won't have room, for example, to use full month names or lengthy product names. A column chart used to make a time-series comparison might suggest a trend that isn't real. Finally, a stacked column chart makes calibrating the second column and any subsequent data series columns very difficult.

Line charts' strengths and limits

Line charts, like the one shown in Figure A-4, work well when you have a large data set to plot. As with area charts, individual data values get plotted as points on a line. For this reason, you're practically unlimited (at least visually) in regard to the number of data values you can plot. Line charts also do a good job of showing trends over time—assuming that a meaningful trend really exists.

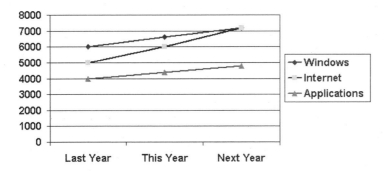

Figure A-4   A line chart.

NOTE   *One other unique strength of line charts in general is that they allow you to use logarithmic scaling. This concept, unfortunately, isn't available for the line charts you produce with Microsoft Graph. However, logarithmic scaling is available for charts you produce with Microsoft Excel. Logarithmic scaling lets you compare relative changes in data series values. Using logarithmic scaling, for example, you could compare the 1980s growth rate in revenues of Microsoft Corporation and International Business Machines Corporation (IBM), even though during the 1980s Microsoft was a much, much smaller company. Normal scaling of such a line chart would obscure the fact that Microsoft was growing at a rate much faster than IBM. By using logarithmic scaling, the relative growth rates in percentage terms become clear.*

Line charts, like every other chart, suffer from limits. A line chart might suggest a trend that doesn't exist or suggest relationships or a correlation between data series that don't exist. If you choose to put symbols along the line to represent the plotted data values, you can't plot many data values without quickly losing legibility because the individual symbol data markers will begin to overwrite each other.

Pie charts' strengths and limits

Pie charts display data in a very simple format. Individual data values get displayed as segments of a circle or slices in a pie, as shown in Figure A-5.

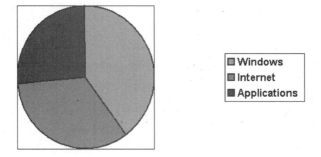

Figure A-5   A pie chart.

Pie charts, for sophisticated business users, don't actually possess many true strengths. Many people argue, in fact, that pie charts should never be used. Whenever you show data values in a pie chart, you will almost always provide more accurate information by simply replacing the pie chart with a table. A pie chart can show only one data series

Figure A-6 shows a table with the same information that appears in a pie chart, as shown in Figure A-5. You would almost always do your audience and chart viewers a service by replacing the pie chart shown in Figure A-5 with the table shown in Figure A-6. The table provides more accurate information.

Windows	6,000,000
Internet	5,000,000
Applications	4,000,000

Figure A-6   A slide with a table that shows the same information as the slide with the pie chart in Figure A-5.

NOTE *In spite of the deficiencies pie charts suffer from, there are special situations in which a pie chart might make sense. Pie charts (children often learn to use them in elementary school) are the most common and easily recognized chart type. Therefore, if you're presenting information to a group of people who might not have experience in viewing and interpreting more sophisticated chart types, you might want or need to use pie charts because you don't have a better option.*

XY charts' strengths and limits

XY, or *scatter*, charts, like the one shown in Figure A-7, probably deliver the most value and information of any chart type you have available. What an XY chart does is plot pairs of points. This process initially sounds complicated, but if you see an example of how it works, it usually becomes very understandable.

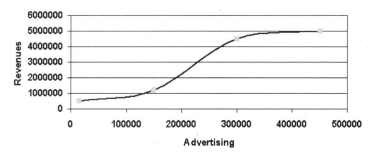

Figure A-7 An XY, or scatter, chart.

Take a look, for example, at the datasheet shown in Figure A-8. This datasheet provides data values that explore the relationship between the amount of money a small firm spends on local advertising and the sales revenue it enjoys—presumably partially as a result.

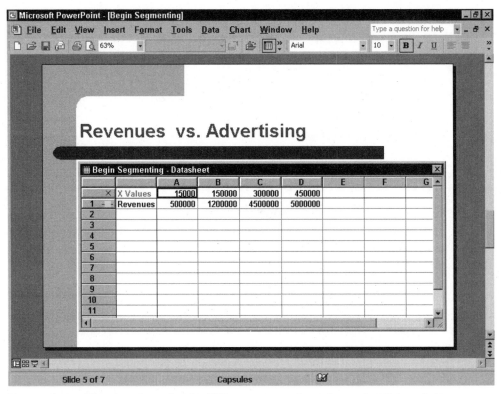

Figure A-8 The datasheet for the XY, or scatter, chart shown in Figure A-7.

NOTE   *The independent variables, or X-values, go into the first row of a datasheet when you're creating an XY chart. In other words, these values replace the data category names.*

Only an XY graph like the one shown in Figure A-7 lets you visually explore this type of relationship. The unique feature that differentiates an XY graph from the other types is that the horizontal axis actually amounts to a second value axis. This value axis in combination with the vertical value axis is used to plot the data. In Figure A-7, for example, what you are really exploring is the relationship of the advertising-expense data values with the revenue data values. In our obviously fictitious example, Figure A-7 shows that initially the advertising expenditures don't seem to have much effect, then they seem to produce a nice boost in sales revenue. But, as the advertising expenditures increase still more, there is a diminishing marginal benefit from the advertising.

XY charts possess a very unique strength: They let you explore the correlation or relationship between two data points. In most people's minds, this is why XY charts represent a superior type of chart. They let your audience or chart viewer visually explore correlation.

Although XY charts don't have the sort of obvious, painful limits that other chart types do, one risk should be mentioned: The fact that an XY, or scatter, chart visually shows the correlation between two data series doesn't mean that a correlation or even a relationship actually exists. If you want to present XY charts in a PowerPoint presentation, you might want to first quantitatively explore the correlation or relationship that exists. You can do regression analysis fairly easily by using Microsoft Excel.

NOTE   *Another book published by Redmond Technology Press,* MBA's Guide to Microsoft Excel, *describes how to use Microsoft Excel for performing regression analysis. This book should be available at any good bookstore and is available from all major online bookstores.*

Doughnut charts' strengths and limits

Doughnut charts, as shown in Figure A-9, plot a data series in concentric rings. Doughnut charts are a way to circumvent the basic problem of using a pie chart, which is that it allows only a single data series. Nonetheless, doughnut charts really suffer from the same limits that pie charts do. You would rarely want to use the doughnut chart, although in some business cultures, doughnut charts are very popular and appear to be generally accepted.

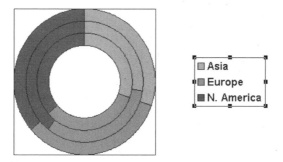

Figure A-9   A doughnut chart.

NOTE   *Identifying a data series in a doughnut chart can be challenging unless you add data labels. In Figure A-9, the first ring is the Windows book sales data series, the second is the Internet book sales data series, and the third is the Applications book sales data series.*

Radar charts' strengths and limits

Radar charts, like the one shown in Figure A-10, possess a unique strength. A radar chart provides a separate value axis for each data category. Because a radar chart does use a separate value axis for each data category, it might be possible to more precisely compare data values within a data category.

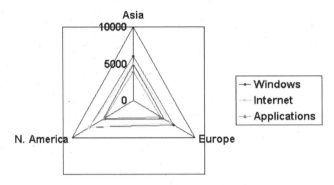

Figure A-10 A radar chart.

A radar chart, predictably, suffers from some limits. You can't easily compare data values in different data categories. This means, for example, that you can't easily show a time-series comparison, nor can you show how data values in a data series change. You can really only make comparisons within a data category. Another possible problem of using a tool like the radar chart is that many people aren't used to seeing and interpreting this chart type. In this case, you obviously reduce the effectiveness of your presentation because you have people not understanding or even misunderstanding your information.

Surface charts' strengths and limits

Three-dimensional *surface* charts represent the most challenging Microsoft Graph chart type to use well. What a surface chart does is plot your data set by using either a two-dimensional or three-dimensional surface, as shown in Figure A-11. In general, the most differentiating and apparent feature of the surface chart is that color is used to show value.

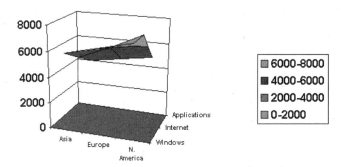

Figure A-11 A surface chart.

The principle challenge in using a surface chart is finding a data set that actually exploits the surface chart's characteristics. We find it difficult, quite candidly, to even think of business examples where a surface chart shows its strength. The only easy-to-grasp example we can come up with is plotting elevations for Mount St. Helens, the local volcano that erupted in our backyard roughly two decades ago. By plotting elevations (assuming that we could find all the data), we could construct a surface chart that resembles the now dormant volcano.

NOTE   *The example of using a surface chart to plot elevation levels for Mount St. Helens also nicely illustrates how you might use color to scale the surface. You could use the color white to depict that portion of the mountain typically covered in snow and use the color green to depict the portion of the mountain that is snow free.*

The unique feature and strength of the surface chart is that this type of chart lets you easily explore relationships both within a data category and within a data series. The surface chart doesn't emphasize data series at the expense of data categories—nor data categories at the expense of data series.

Surface charts, predictably, suffer from some limits. Perhaps the most important one to note is that there is not a generally agreed-on way to use color to denote value. Is green bigger than blue? Is yellow less than red? You see the problem.

One other issue relates to the three-dimensional surface chart types. Obviously, with a three-dimensional surface chart, it is possible that some portion of the surface will be obscured. Peaks might obscure valleys.

Bubble charts' strengths and limits

A *bubble chart,* like the one shown in Figure A-12, amounts to a sort of supercharged XY graph. As you might recall from this Appendix's earlier discussion, an XY, or scatter, chart lets you compare two sets of data values by using both the horizontal and vertical axes as values axes. A bubble chart does the same thing. In addition, however, it lets you incorporate a third set of data values, and this third set of data values determines the size of the bubble data marker used in the chart.

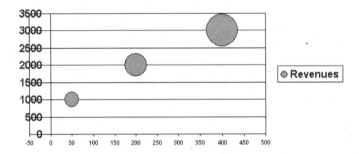

Figure A-12   A bubble chart.

A bubble chart theoretically offers you the same advantages as an XY chart. However, the third data series—the one that sizes the bubbles on your chart—might overcomplicate the chart. It seems very likely that this rather exotic chart type might be one that is too unusual or unfamiliar for most audiences.

Figure A-13 shows the data sheet for the bubble chart shown in Figure A-12. Note that the last row of the datasheet provides the values that determine the size of the bubbles.

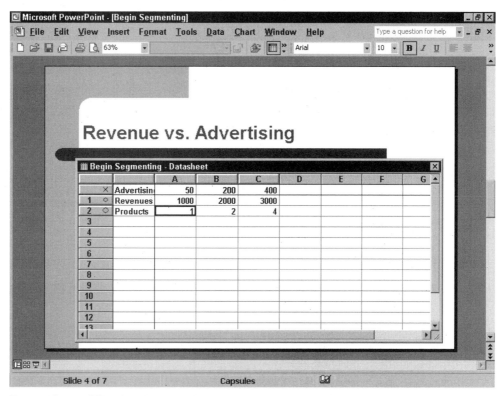

Figure A-13 The datasheet used for the bubble chart shown in Figure A-12.

Stock charts' strengths and limits

The *stock* chart lets you depict stock price and volume information in a high, low, and close chart, as shown in Figure A-14. A stock chart is really just a column chart; as a result, it possesses the same strengths and limits as column charts.

NOTE   *You can sometimes use a stock chart to depict other data sets. We've seen stock charts used to show weather data, such as the temperature at dawn, noon, and dusk. Sometimes stock charts, particularly because many business users understand them, can be a very useful addition to your repertoire of graphing tools.*

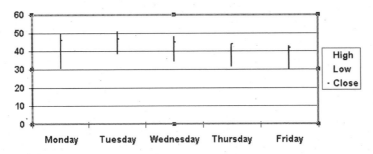

Figure A-14 A high-low-close stock chart.

Note that Microsoft Graph expects stock price data to be arranged in high-low-close order if you're plotting the daily high, daily low, and closing price, as shown in Figure A-15. (If you're plotting the opening price too, Microsoft Graph expects stock price data to be arranged in high-low-open-close order.)

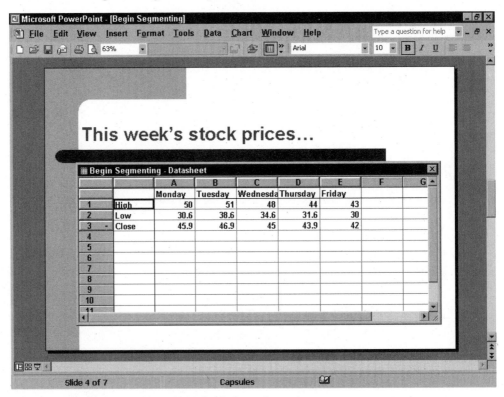

Figure A-15 The datasheet for a high-low-close chart.

Cylinder, cone, and pyramid charts' strengths and limits

The remaining three chart types that Microsoft Graph supplies are *cylinder* charts, *cone* charts, and *pyramid* charts. These three chart types are really all the same. The only thing that differs from one chart type to the next is the type of data marker used as shown in Figure A-16. Really, these charts are all simply three-dimensional column charts—except that the columns have been replaced. The cylinder chart doesn't use columns—it uses cylinders; the cone chart type doesn't use columns—it uses cones; and the pyramid chart type doesn't use columns—it uses pyramids.

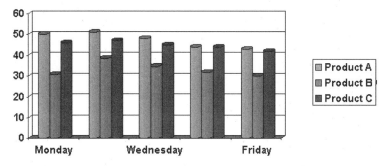

Figure A-16 A cylinder chart.

Because the cylinder, cone, and pyramid chart types resemble the column chart type, they predictably possess the same strengths and limits that the column chart does.

Avoiding Common Charting Mistakes

You can unfortunately make many serious mistakes in constructing charts for a presentation. Nevertheless, by applying some common sense, you can avoid the most common and most serious mistakes.

Using the wrong chart type

The most common charting mistake must be using the wrong chart type. You really do want to keep in mind the essential data comparison you want to make on your chart. After you know which type of data comparison you want to make, you should consider only those chart types that emphasize or support the essential data comparison.

Using the dimension of depth inappropriately

A more controversial charting mistake, in our opinion, is the inappropriate use of a third dimension. By adding a third dimension, you do add visual interest to your charts. The third dimension of depth tends to make your charts look richer—and that is appealing, at least on a gut level. However, there is a problem with adding depth to charts: You lose visual precision. This almost always means that chart viewers will find it more difficult to precisely compare the data markers. Three-dimensional bars and columns are challenging to use for comparisons, and three-dimensional lines and area charts are almost impossible to use for comparison.

NOTE   *An old rule of thumb about creating charts is this: Your chart shouldn't have more dimensions than your data. For this reason, if we were preparing charts for a presentation, we would stick with two-dimensional charts. Invariably, your data set will show only two dimensions, and therefore, your chart should use only two dimensions. If we were presenting information to an audience viewing many other presentations using three-dimensional graphics, we might even consider stating that our presentation used only two-dimensional charts to make them more precise.*

Creating phantom data markers

A third charting mistake is the problem of other nearby graphics objects being perhaps subconsciously included as part of the chart. For example, look at the chart shown in Figure A-17. This simple slide, artificial in its construct, consists of three columns and a legend.

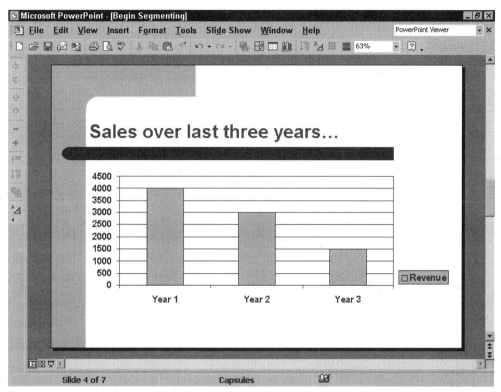

Figure A-17 A chart that includes a phantom data marker.

If you take a critical look at the chart shown in Figure A-17, you'll see that something curious is happening: The legend box that's about the same color as the chart data markers almost without realization amounts to a fourth data marker—and thereby probably overstates the chart's message. The three data markers that are part of the chart show that the values are dropping over time, but the legend box acts like a fourth phantom data marker that overstates this trend and amplifies it in the viewer's mind.

Appendix B

USING WORDART

Featuring:

- Creating a WordArt Object
- Working with WordArt Objects on a Slide
- Using the WordArt Toolbar

As mentioned in "Step 3: Add Objects," you can turn text into a graphics object. To do this, you use the WordArt applet. WordArt, like Microsoft Graph, is a small program that comes with PowerPoint.

Creating a WordArt Object

To create a piece of text using WordArt, take the following steps:

1. **Start the WordArt applet.**

   Choose the Insert menu's Picture command, and then choose the WordArt command from the Picture submenu. When you do, PowerPoint starts the WordArt program. The first window you'll see is the WordArt Gallery, shown in Figure B-1. This window shows you the various ways you can display the selected text as a graphics image.

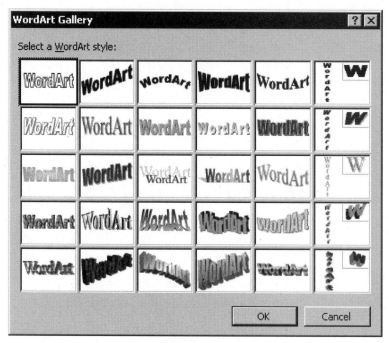

Figure B-1 The WordArt Gallery window.

2. Select the WordArt style that looks like how you want your object to look.

To select a WordArt style, click on the images shown on the WordArt Gallery window. Then click OK. WordArt displays the Edit WordArt Text window, as shown in Figure B-2.

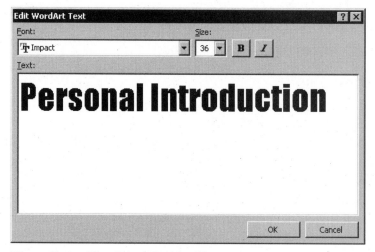

Figure B-2 The Edit WordArt Text window.

3. **Enter the text.**

Use the Edit WordArt Text window to enter the text you want to turn into a WordArt object.

4. **Select the font.**

When WordArt displays the Edit WordArt Text window, use the Font list box to select the font you want to use. You can click the button at the right end of the Font list box to display a list of available fonts. The Text box shows you how your font selection looks—this is the preview area beneath the Font and Size boxes and the Bold and Italic buttons.

5. **Select a point size.**

Use the Size box to specify the point size you want WordArt to use for the text. One point equals 1/72 inch. So, if you want your WordArt text object to measure 1 inch tall, set the size box to 72 points. If you want the size to measure ½ inch in height, set the Size box to 36 points.

6. **As desired, add boldfacing and italicization.**

You can click the Bold and Italic buttons that appear to the right of the Font and Size boxes, to boldface or italicize the text. The Bold and Italic buttons are toggle switches: To un-bold and un-italicize the text, click the buttons again.

7. **Add the WordArt object to your slide.**

After you've specified the font, size, and any boldfacing and italicization, click the OK button. WordArt adds the WordArt object to the PowerPoint slide.

NOTE *You can double-click the new WordArt image to redisplay the Edit WordArt window. This time, however, it provides a Preview button. You can click the Preview button to see what your WordArt style or text looks like on the slide. You may need to move the window to see the preview image on the slide.*

Working with WordArt Objects on a Slide

After WordArt adds the object to the PowerPoint slide, as shown in Figure B-3, you can move and resize the object by clicking and dragging. To correctly position the WordArt object, drag it to the appropriate location. To resize the object, drag the selection handles that surround the object. To change the WordArt effect, you can also typically drag the yellow diamond marker. You would drag this marker, for example, to make a leaning WordArt object lean more or lean less.

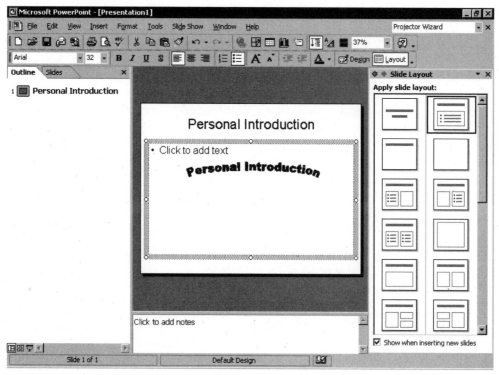

Figure B-3   A WordArt object on a slide.

Using the WordArt Toolbar

You can use the WordArt toolbar to make additional changes to the WordArt object. Figure B-4 shows the WordArt toolbar. The following paragraphs briefly describe what each of the toolbar buttons does.

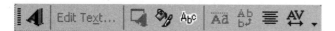

Figure B-4   The WordArt toolbar.

NOTE   *If you point to a toolbar button, WordArt displays the toolbar button's name. For example, if you point to the first toolbar button on the WordArt toolbar or the one that shows a big letter A tipping over, you see the ToolTip, Insert WordArt. It indicates that the tool's name is Insert WordArt.*

Inserting another WordArt object

The Insert WordArt button displays the WordArt Gallery window, as shown in Figure B-1. You can click this button if you want to add another new WordArt object to the slide.

Editing WordArt text

The Edit Text tool redisplays the Edit WordArt Text window, as shown in Figure B-2. You can use this window, as discussed earlier, to change the font, size, boldface, and italics specifications for the WordArt object. You can also use this window's Text box to edit the text used to create the WordArt object.

Changing the WordArt Gallery setting

The third button, the WordArt Gallery button, lets you select a new gallery setting for the existing, selected WordArt object. If you click this button, WordArt displays a WordArt Gallery window similar to the WordArt Gallery window shown in Figure B-1. (This window differs from the one shown in Figure B-1, however, in that it provides a Preview button.)

Formatting WordArt objects

The WordArt toolbar provides several buttons you can use to change the appearance of your WordArt objects. The Format WordArt button on the WordArt toolbar lets you change the color used for the WordArt object; the line, color, and style used to draw the WordArt object; and the size and layout of the WordArt object.

When you choose the Format WordArt button, WordArt displays the dialog box shown in Figure B-5. You can use its Colors And Lines tab to change, predictably, the color and lines used to create the WordArt object. To make changes, simply use the tab's drop-down list boxes to select different colors, line styles, and so on.

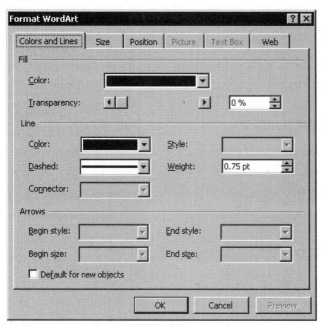

Figure B-5 The Colors And Lines tab.

You can use the Size tab, as shown in Figure B-6, to change the dimensions of the WordArt object.

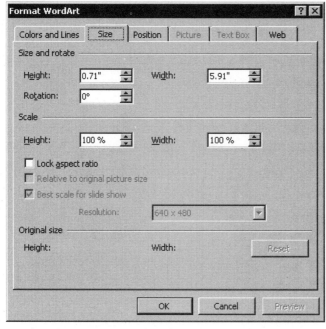

Figure B-6 The Size tab.

You can use the Position tab, shown in Figure B-7, to describe how the WordArt object should be positioned on a page in relation to other objects.

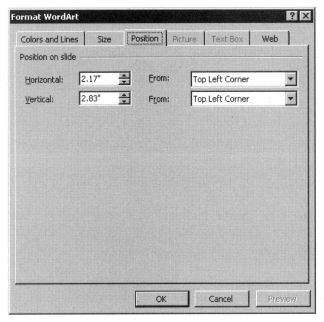

Figure B-7   The Position tab.

The other tabs in the Format WordArt dialog box work in a similar fashion. Not every tab will be available, however. Some tabs make sense only in certain situations.

The WordArt Shape button displays a menu of pictures you can choose from to select the shape of the WordArt object, as shown in Figure B-8. You simply click the shape you want the WordArt object to take.

Figure B-8   The WordArt Shape menu displayed in the PowerPoint window.

The WordArt Same Letter Heights tool lets you tell WordArt that each letter in the WordArt graphics image should be the same height. The WordArt Same Letter Heights button is a toggle switch. If you click it again, WordArt resizes the letter heights back to their original sizes.

The WordArt Vertical Text toolbar lets you flip the WordArt text so that it's vertical rather than horizontal. WordArt also adds selection handles after you click the tool. You can use these selection handles to rotate the object.

The WordArt Alignment button displays a menu of text-alignment options, as shown in Figure B-9. You simply select the menu command that refers to the text alignment you want to use for text in the WordArt object.

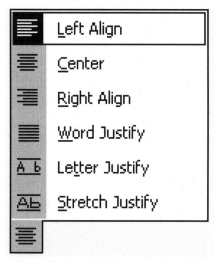

Figure B-9   The Text Alignment menu displayed in the PowerPoint window.

The WordArt Character Spacing tool, the last one on the toolbar, displays a menu of character-spacing commands, as shown in Figure B-10. You choose the character-spacing command that refers to the type of spacing you want for the text that makes the WordArt object.

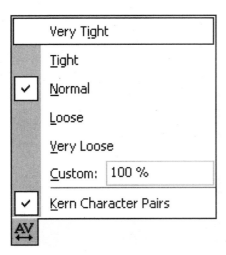

Figure B-10 The Character Spacing menu displayed in the PowerPoint window.

To remove the WordArt toolbar, simply click some other object on the PowerPoint slide to select it. If the WordArt object isn't selected, PowerPoint removes the WordArt toolbar. If you later want to make additional changes to the WordArt object, simply click the WordArt object again. PowerPoint will reopen the WordArt toolbar. You can use its buttons to make whatever changes you want.

Appendix C

CUSTOMIZING POWERPOINT

Featuring:

- Customizing Options
- Customizing Toolbars and Menus
- Reviewing the Macro and Visual Basic Features

Appropriately, this last Appendix of the book is about customizing the way that the PowerPoint program works and looks. Most executive users will never need or want to take the time to make the sorts of changes that this Appendix describes. However, a handful of users will, and so the following paragraphs describe how to use the Tools menu's Options and Customize commands to do these things.

NOTE   *The last paragraphs of this Appendix also briefly discuss macros and Visual Basic.*

Customizing Options

Most of the changes that you make to the PowerPoint program you make using the Options dialog box. To display this dialog box, you start PowerPoint and choose the Tools menu's Options command.

The Options dialog box provides six tabs: View, General, Edit, Print, Save, and Spelling And Style. Each tab provides boxes and buttons you use to make a certain category of changes, or customizations. The Print tab, for example, lets you make changes to the way PowerPoint prints presentations.

Changing the View settings

The View tab (see Figure C-1) lets you control how the PowerPoint window shows its components and how the Slide Show window displays a presentation. (The Slide Show window is what an actual slide show appears in.)

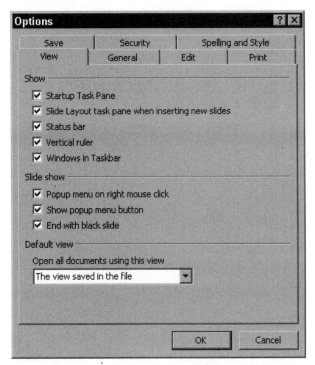

Figure C-1   The View tab of the Options dialog box.

The bulleted list that follows explains what each of the View tab's options do:

- The Startup task pane check box lets you tell PowerPoint whether you want to see the New Presentation task pane each time you start PowerPoint. The New Presentation task pane is the one you use to tell PowerPoint whether you want to create a new presentation using the AutoContent Wizard, based on a design template, or using just a blank presentation.

- The Slide Layout task pane When Inserting New Slides check box lets you tell PowerPoint that you want the Slide Layout task pane displayed each time you insert a new slide into a presentation. The Slide Layout task pane, displays a set of slide layouts you can choose from. (A slide layout is just a slide template with one or more object placeholders.)

- The Status Bar box lets you tell PowerPoint to display the status bar at the bottom of the PowerPoint program window. The status bar displays information about the PowerPoint program and active presentation and slide.

- The Vertical Ruler box lets you tell PowerPoint that it should display the vertical ruler in the PowerPoint window when the horizontal ruler is displayed. You display the rulers in order to more precisely align and position objects. To display a ruler, use the View menu's Ruler command.

- The Windows In Taskbar box lets you tell Windows that each open PowerPoint presentation should have its own button on the Windows taskbar.

- The Popup Menu On Right Mouse Click box lets you tell PowerPoint that during a slide show, right-clicking the slide should display a popup Shortcuts menu of commands. This menu includes commands for moving from slide to slide, for using presentation tools like the Meeting Minder, and for controlling how the mouse pointer looks and works during the slide show.

- The Show Popup Menu Button box lets you tell PowerPoint to put a button in the lower left corner of slides during a slide show. This button can be clicked to display the popup Shortcuts menu, too.

- The End With Black Slide box lets you tell PowerPoint whether it should end presentations with an empty black slide. (Usually you do want to do this since the alternative is to display the PowerPoint program window.)

- The Open All Documents Using This View list box lets you tell PowerPoint what view it should use to display a presentation that is opened.

Obviously, marking one of the View tab's boxes with a check turns on the feature described. And unmarking the box turns off the feature.

Changing the General settings

The General tab (see Figure C-2) provides a space for customization options that are unrelated to the other tabs of the Options dialog box.

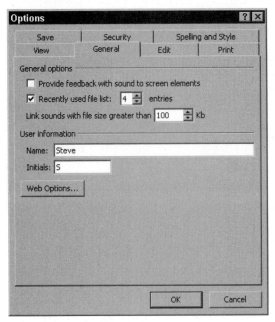

Figure C-2 The General tab of the Options dialog box.

The General Options area of the General tab provides the options described in the bulleted list that follows:

- The Provide Feedback With Sound To Screen Elements box lets you tell PowerPoint whether it (and other Office programs like Word and Excel) should play sounds as part of the user interface and experience. For example, when this box is checked, PowerPoint plays a sound when a message box appears.

- The Recently Used File List checkbox and text box let you tell PowerPoint how many recently used presentations it should list at the bottom of the File menu. To add recently used presentations to the File menu, you check the box. To tell PowerPoint how many recently used files it should list, you enter a value into the Entries text box.

- The Link Sounds With File Size Greater Than [X] Kb text box lets you set a size limit for sound files that are stored with the presentation. Sound files greater than the specified size in Kb (kilobytes) are not stored with the presentation file but are instead independently stored as separate files. To connect the sound file to the presentation file, PowerPoint uses a file link.

- The User Information provides Name and Initials boxes that PowerPoint uses to identify the person creating and modifying a presentation. (To see user name and initials information for a presentation, choose the File menu's Properties command and click the Statistics tab.)

The Web Options button, if clicked, displays a whole new dialog box with options that let you control how slides you're showing as web pages appear (see Figure C-3).

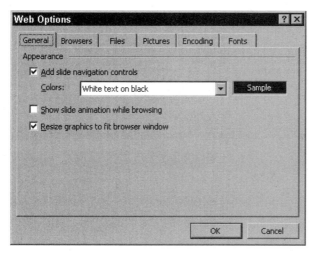

Figure C-3   The General tab of the Web Options dialog box.

The Web Options dialog box's General tab (see Figure C-3) includes check boxes for controlling the overall appearance of your slide web pages:

- The Add Slide Navigation Controls box and Colors list box let you tell PowerPoint that it should create web-page versions of slides that include an Outline pane and Notes pane. The Colors list box, of course, lets you tell PowerPoint what color it should use for the text and background areas of the Outline and Notes panes.

- The Slide Show Animation While Browsing box lets you tell PowerPoint that it should use any slide animation and transitions that you've added to the presentation. Note that someone viewing the presentation needs to be using version 4.0 or later 'of Microsoft's Internet Explorer browser in order to see these animation effects.

- The Resize Graphics To Fit Browser Window box lets you tell PowerPoint to size graphics so they appear proportional on web pages. Again, note that someone viewing the presentation needs to be using version 4.0 or later of Microsoft's Internet Explorer browser in order for graphic resizing to work.

The Web Option's Browsers tab (see Figure C-4) lets you identify the web browser that people will use to view the presentation:

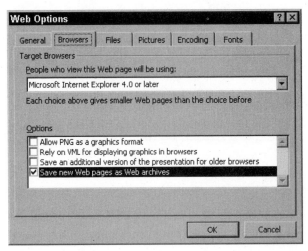

Figure C-4 The Browsers tab of the Web Options dialog box.

- Select the web browser from the People Who View This Web Page Will Be Using list box. (The list box provides selections for all recent versions of Microsoft Internet Explorer and Netscape Navigator.)

- The Allow PNG As A Graphics Format box tells PowerPoint to use the Portable Network Graphics format for pictures on your web pages. Pictures that use the Portable Network Graphics format take less time to create than lowest-common-denominator picture formats like JPEG, but before using them you should confirm that your network supports them.

- The Rely On VML For Displaying Graphics In Browsers box lets you tell PowerPoint that it can use Vector Markup Language for displaying graphic images. Using Vector Markup Language lets you more quickly create web presentations because PowerPoint doesn't have to regenerate graphic images in a lowest-common-denominator format. However, to use Vector Markup Language, you should be using version 5.0 or later of Microsoft's Internet Explorer web browser.

- The Save An Additional Version of The Presentation For Older Browsers check box lets you create a special version of a web presentation that will work with old web browsers.

- The Save New Web Pages As Web Archives check box lets you save presentations to the web as archives.

The Web Options dialog box's Files tab (see Figure C-5) includes check boxes for specifying how PowerPoint organizes the files that are necessary to create web pages:

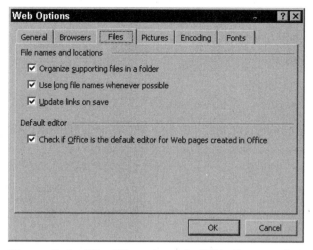

Figure C-5   The Files tab of the Web Options dialog box.

- The Organize Supporting Files In A Folder box tells PowerPoint to collect all of the component files necessary to construct web pages in a separate folder. Note that each of the graphical elements used on a slide actually need to be separate files to construct the web page, so you do want these components stored together.

- The Use Long File Names Whenever Possible box tells PowerPoint it is okay to use long filenames when saving your web presentation to the web server. (If you unmark this check box, PowerPoint uses eight-character filenames.)

- The Update Links On Save box tells PowerPoint to automatically update any file linking information when you save the presentation.

- The Default Editor box lets you tell PowerPoint that you'll use PowerPoint or another Office program like Microsoft Word or Microsoft FrontPage to make changes to web pages you create using PowerPoint.

The Web Options dialog box's Pictures tab (see Figure C-6) provides a list box for specifying how PowerPoint should handle any pictures. Use the Screen Size drop-down list box to indicate what screen resolution you want to tailor your web pages for.

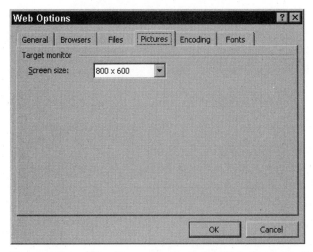

Figure C-6   The Pictures tab of the Web Options dialog box.

The Web Options dialog box's Encoding tab (see Figure C-7) includes check boxes for specifying which language code PowerPoint should use for the web pages:

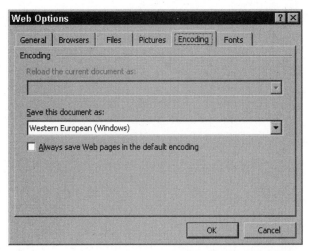

Figure C-7   The Encoding tab of the Web Options dialog box.

- The Reload The Current Document As drop-down list lets you select another language code and use it for the web page document.

- The Save This Document As drop-down list box lets you choose the language code that PowerPoint should use for creating a web page document.

- The Always Save Web Pages In The Default Encoding box lets you tell PowerPoint that it should save all web page documents in whatever language code shows in the Save This Document As drop-down list box.

The Web Options dialog box's Fonts tab (see Figure C-8) includes boxes for specifying which fonts PowerPoint should use for the web pages:

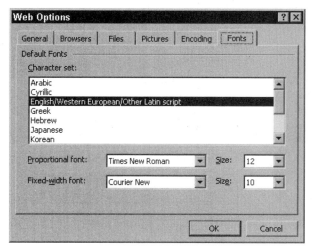

Figure C-8   The Fonts tab of the Web Options dialog box.

- The Character Set box lets you tell PowerPoint which character set it should use. (Except in obvious cases, you probably want to use the English/Western European/Other Latin Script character set.)

- The Proportional Font boxes let you tell PowerPoint which font and point size PowerPoint should use for any proportional fonts on web pages.

- The Fixed-Width Font boxes let you tell PowerPoint which font and point size it should use for fixed-width fonts.

NOTE   *Characters in a proportional font vary in width—an* m, *for example, is wider than an* i. *In a fixed width font, however, all characters have the same width— an* m *would have the same width as an* i.

Changing the Edit settings

The Edit tab of the Options dialog box (see Figure C-9) lets you control how PowerPoint's editing tools work and it provides a text box for specifying how many editing actions you can undo.

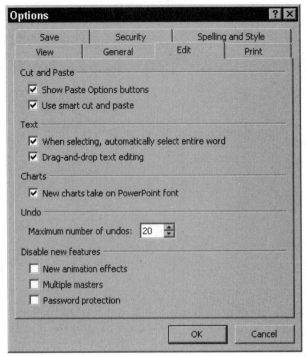

Figure C-9 The Edit tab of the Options dialog box.

The Edit tab provides the options described in the bulleted list that follows:

- The Show Paste Options Button box lets you tell PowerPoint to display a Paste button that lets you specify how data should be pasted into a slide.

- The Use Smart Cut And Paste box tells PowerPoint that it should attempt to remove extra, unneeded spaces and add any needed spaces when you delete and insert text.

- The When Selecting, Automatically Select Entire Word box lets you tell PowerPoint that when you select text, PowerPoint should first assume you want to select whole word plus the space after the word.

- The Drag-And-Drop Text Editing box tells PowerPoint that you want to enable drag-and-drop editing so you can move and copy text and images by dragging the mouse.

- The New Charts Take On PowerPoint Font box tells PowerPoint that any charts you add to a presentation should use the PowerPoint fonts rather than those that may have been specified using the program used to create the chart.

- The Maximum Number Of Undos box tells PowerPoint how many editing actions you want to be able to undo. More is usually better, but the greater the number the more memory PowerPoint needs to remember the changes you've made.

- The Disable New Features check boxes—New Animation Effects, Multiple Masters, and Password Protection—let you turn off the corresponding new features.

Changing the Print settings

The Print tab (see Figure C-10) lets you control the way PowerPoint prints presentations.

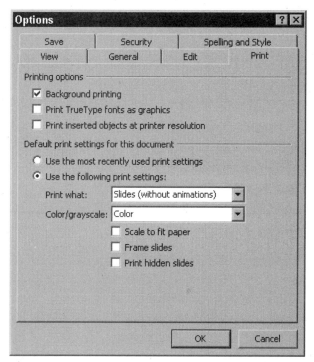

Figure C-10 The Print tab of the Options dialog box.

The Print tab provides the options described in the bulleted list that follows:

- The Background Printing box lets you tell PowerPoint to print in the background so that even as PowerPoint is printing you can continue to work with the PowerPoint program and your presentations.

- The Print TrueType Fonts As Graphics box lets you tell PowerPoint how it should handle TrueType fonts in your presentation. Most often, you want to print these fonts as fonts and so will leave the box unmarked. If you're printing to a printer that doesn't support TrueType fonts, however, you can mark this check box to tell PowerPoint it should print the fonts as if they're graphic images.

- The Print Inserted Objects At Printer Resolution box lets you tell PowerPoint to print objects at the printer's presumably lower resolution.

- The Use The Most Recently Used Print Settings button lets you tell PowerPoint that if you click the toolbar's Print button, it should just print the presentation using whatever print settings you last used.

- The Use The Following Default Print Settings option button lets you tell PowerPoint that it should use some other set of print settings when you click the Print toolbar button. To specify these print settings, you use the Print What drop-down list box, the Color/Grayscale list box, and the check boxes that appear beneath the Color/Grayscale drop-down list box.

Changing the Save Settings

The Save tab (see Figure C-11) lets you control the way PowerPoint saves your presentations.

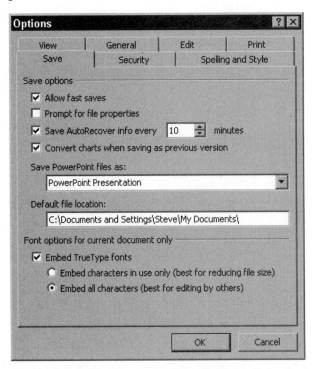

Figure C-11 The Save tab of the Options dialog box.

The Save tab provides the options described in the bulleted list that follows:

- The Allow Fast Saves box lets you tell PowerPoint that it should use its fast-save capability. A "fast" file save is faster than a regular file save because in a fast save PowerPoint saves only the new changes to the presentation file. Files created by a "fast" file save are usually larger than files created by a regular file save, however.

- The Prompt For File Properties box lets you tell PowerPoint that it should display the Summary tab of the properties dialog box when you first save a presentation. The Summary tab of the properties dialog box, which can also be displayed by choosing the File menu's Properties command, lets you store general information about the presentation file such as a title, subject, and author.

- The Save AutoRecover Info Every [X] Minutes check box and text box let you turn on PowerPoint's AutoRecover feature and specify how often AutoRecover saves recovery information. If AutoRecover is turned on, PowerPoint saves changes at the specified interval in minutes. Should your computer or the PowerPoint program stop working, the next time PowerPoint start it opens the AutoRecover file. With its information you may be able to recover your last work.

- The Convert Charts When Saving As Previous Version box lets you tell PowerPoint that when you save a presentation using an earlier PowerPoint file format (presumably so you can work with the presentation using an earlier version of PowerPoint) that it should convert any charts used in a presentation to an earlier, usable format, too.

- The Save PowerPoint Files As box lets you tell PowerPoint which file format it should suggest you use when saving presentations. This suggested file format appears in the Save Files As Type box on the Save dialog box. The Save dialog box appears when you choose the File menu's Save As command.

- The Default File Location box tells PowerPoint where it should suggest saving presentations. This suggested file location appears in the Save In box on the Save dialog box. The Save dialog box appears when you choose the File menu's Save As command.

NOTE   *When you make a change to the default file format or the default file location using the Save PowerPoint Files As box or the Default File Location box, the change doesn't take effect until the next time you start PowerPoint.*

- The Embed TrueType Fonts check box lets you include the TrueType fonts with your presentation so that text will display correctly on other computers even if the other computers don't have the fonts.

The Security tab, shown in Figure C-12, lets you protect a presentation by adding passwords:

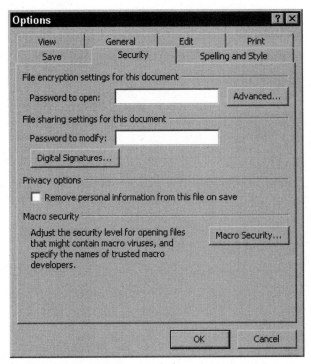

Figure C-12 The Security tab of the Option dialog box.

- The Password To Open box lets you enter a password that must be supplied in order to open a presentation. (For extra security, you can click the Advanced button and select the type of file encryption you want to use.)

- The Password To Modify box lets you enter a password that must be supplied in order to save changes to the presentation. (You can also click the Digital Signatures button to add digital signatures to the presentation when people save changes.)

- The Remove Personal Information From This File On Save tells PowerPoint *not* to save information about the person saving the file with the other file properties.

- The Macro Security button displays a dialog box you use to control whether PowerPoint will run macros and if so whose macros will run.

Changing the Spelling And Style settings

The Spelling And Style tab (see Figure C-13) lets you exercise control over the way that PowerPoint checks the spelling in your presentation, alerts you to misspellings, and helps you fix spelling and style errors.

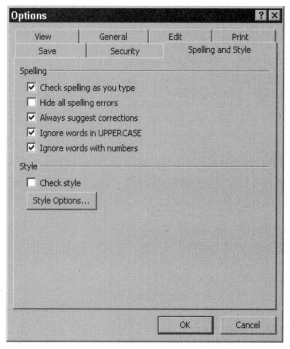

Figure C-13 The Spelling And Style tab of the Options dialog box.

The Spelling Errors And Style tab provides the options described in the bulleted list that follows:

- The Check Spelling As You Type box tells PowerPoint that it should spell-check words as you type them.

- The Hide All Spelling Errors tells PowerPoint that it should not point out misspelled words by underlining them with a wavy red line. By default, this option is not turned on, so PowerPoint does indeed point out misspellings in this manner.

- The Always Suggest Corrections box tells PowerPoint that it should suggest corrections for misspelled words when you right-click the misspelling. PowerPoint provides suggested corrections by listing them on the Shortcuts menu that appears when you right-click the misspelled word.

- The Ignore Words In UPPERCASE box tells PowerPoint that it shouldn't attempt to check the spelling of words that appear in all uppercase letters. The reason for this option is that often, words that appear in all uppercase letters aren't really words at all but acronyms and abbreviations.

- The Ignore Words With Numbers box tells PowerPoint that it shouldn't attempt to check the spelling of words that use numbers. The reason for this is that almost always, chunks of text that use numbers aren't words but identifiers—things like product codes, account numbers, and so forth.

- The Check Style box tells PowerPoint that it should check the presentation's styles for consistency and also that it should automatically correct spelling, capitalization and punctuation.

To control how PowerPoint checks styles, you click the Style Options button. When you do, PowerPoint displays the Style Options dialog box. The Style Options dialog box provides two tabs you use for controlling style checking: Case And End Punctuation (see Figure C-14) and Visual Clarity (see Figure C-15).

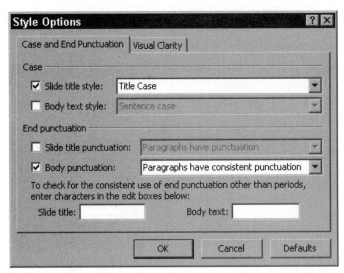

Figure C-14 The Case And End Punctuation tab of the Style Options dialog box.

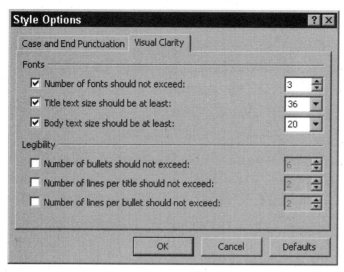

Figure C-15 The Visual Clarity tab of the Style Options dialog box.

The Case And End Punctuation tab of the Style Options dialog box (see Figure C-14) provides the options described in the bulleted list that follows:

- The Slide Title Style boxes tell PowerPoint that it should check the capitalization of slide titles. To have PowerPoint perform this check, mark the Slide Title Style box. To specify what type of capitalization slide titles should use, select a capitalization style from the Slide Title Style drop-down list box.

- The Body Text Style boxes tell PowerPoint that it should check the capitalization of slide text such as text used in bulleted lists. To have PowerPoint perform this check, mark the Body Text Style box. To specify what type of capitalization slide text should use, select a capitalization style from the Body Text Style drop-down list box.

- The Slide Title Punctuation boxes tell PowerPoint that it should check the ending punctuation of slide titles. To have PowerPoint perform this check, mark the Slide Title Punctuation box. To specify what type of ending punctuation slide titles should use, select an ending punctuation style from the Slide Title Punctuation drop-down list box.

- The Body Punctuation boxes tell PowerPoint that it should check the ending punctuation of slide body text such as the text in bulleted lists. To have PowerPoint perform this check, mark the Body Punctuation box. To specify what type of ending punctuation body text should use, select an ending punctuation style from the Body Punctuation drop-down list box.

If the ending punctuation for slide titles and body text should be something other than a period, use the Slide Title and Body Text boxes to supply the correct ending punctuation symbol or character.

The Visual Clarity tab of the Style Options dialog box (see Figure C-15) provides the options described in the bulleted list that follows:

- The Number Of Fonts Should Not Exceed boxes tell PowerPoint to limit the number of fonts used in your presentation. Mark the check box to have PowerPoint perform this style check. Specify the maximum number of fonts that should be used by entering a value into the text box.

- The Title Text Size Should Be At Least boxes tell PowerPoint how large slide title text should be. Mark the check box to have PowerPoint perform this style check. Specify the title point size by entering a value into the text box. (The initial title text size setting is 36 points, or one-half inch.)

- The Body Text Size Should Be At Least boxes tell PowerPoint how large body text should be. Mark the check box to have PowerPoint perform this style check. Specify the body text point size by entering a value into the text box.

- The Number Of Bullets Should Not Exceed boxes tell PowerPoint how many points can be in a bulleted list. Mark the check box to have PowerPoint perform this style check. Specify the maximum number of bullet points by entering a value into the text box.

- The Number Of Lines Per Title Should Not Exceed boxes tell PowerPoint how many lines of text can be used in a slide title. Mark the check box to have PowerPoint perform this style check. Specify the maximum number of lines by entering a value into the text box.

- The Number Of Lines Per Bullet Should Not Exceed boxes tell PowerPoint how many lines of text can be in a bullet point. Mark the check box to have PowerPoint perform this style check. Specify the maximum number of lines by entering a value into the text box.

Customizing Toolbars and Menus

You can customize PowerPoint's toolbars and menus. To make these sorts of changes, you choose the Tools menu's Customize command. When you choose this command, PowerPoint displays the Customize dialog box. The Customize dialog box provides three tabs: Toolbars, which you use to make changes to toolbars, predictably, Commands which you use to review menus and their commands, and Options which you use to control the way that toolbars and menus work.

Customizing toolbars

To make changes to PowerPoint's toolbars, you use the Toolbars tab of the Customize dialog box (see Figure C-16).

Figure C-16 The Toolbars tab of the Customize dialog box.

The Toolbars list box lets you specify which toolbars should always appear in the PowerPoint window. (Those toolbars marked with checks appear, those that are unmarked don't appear.)

You can create a new toolbar by clicking the New button and providing a name for the new toolbar using the New Toolbar dialog box (see Figure C-17). To add tools to the new toolbar, first display the new (and initially empty) toolbar. Then drag tools from other toolbars to the new toolbar.

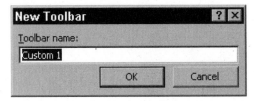

Figure C-17 The New Toolbar dialog box.

Using the Toolbars tab, you can rename a toolbar you create by selecting it in the Toolbars list box, clicking the Rename button, and then entering a new name when PowerPoint displays the Rename Toolbar dialog box (see Figure C-18).

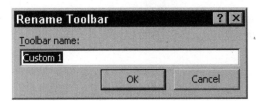

Figure C-18 The Rename Toolbar dialog box.

You can remove a toolbar you create by selecting it in the Toolbars list box and then clicking the Delete button.

You can undo your changes to toolbars by clicking the Reset button.

Using the Commands tab

While you might expect to use the Commands tab of the Customize dialog box to make changes to PowerPoint's menus (see Figure C-19), you actually can't. You can use the tab, however, to see the help description that appears in the status bar when you highlight some menu or command. To do this, select the menu from the Categories list box, select the command from the Commands list box, and then click the Description button.

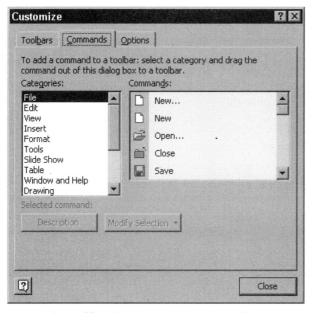

Figure C-19 The Commands tab of the Customize dialog box.

Customizing toolbar and menu options

To make changes to the way that PowerPoint's toolbar and menus work, you use the Options tab of the Customize dialog box (see Figure C-20).

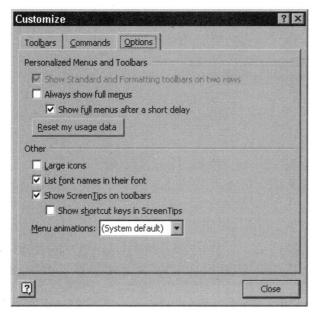

Figure C-20 The Options tab of the Customize dialog box.

The Options tab provides the options described in the bulleted list that follows:

- The Show Standard And Formatting Toolbars On Two Rows box tells PowerPoint to use two separate toolbars for the Standard and Formatting toolbars.

- The Always Show Full Menus box tells PowerPoint that it should not personalize menus by at first showing only the commands you've recently used.

- The Reset My Usage Data button tells PowerPoint to start over in its analysis of which commands you've recently or are frequently using. This analysis is what PowerPoint uses to determine which commands go onto menus when you've marked Always Show Full Menus.

- The Large Icons box tells PowerPoint to use large icons and buttons for toolbar tools.

- The List Font Names In Their Font box tells PowerPoint to use the font for listing the font in places like the Font menu. (When this option is turned on, the Times New Roman font selection in a list box appears in the Times New Roman font.)

- The Show ScreenTips On Toolbars box tells PowerPoint to display tool names in popup boxes when you point to tools. If you've turned on the Show ScreenTips On Toolbars feature, you can also tell PowerPoint to provide shortcut information with the ScreenTips by marking the Show Shortcut Keys In ScreenTips box.

- The Menu Animations drop-down list box lets you specify whether PowerPoint should use animation on its menus and if so what type of animation you want.

Reviewing the Macro and Visual Basic Features

A short book like this one isn't the place to describe macros or the Visual Basic programming language. However, before closing this book, let us briefly point out that PowerPoint does allow users to create and use macros and Visual Basic modules.

A macro, essentially, is a just a recorded set of keystrokes that can be played back. For often-repeated or lengthy keystroke sequences, macros can be real timesavers, although their utility for PowerPoint users is probably limited. Most of the work with PowerPoint is, mechanically speaking, quite simple. (This often isn't the case if you're talking about a complex program like Microsoft Word or Microsoft Excel.)

Visual Basic for Applications is a variant of Microsoft's popular Visual Basic programming language, which, in turn, is a variant of the Basic programming language. Visual Basic, essentially, lets create programs that run alongside the PowerPoint program. In a sense, then, Visual Basic means can use PowerPoint as a development platform for creating still other programs. However, using Visual Basic requires programming knowledge and skills.

GLOSSARY

Animated gif

An animated gif is an image file that shows movement. You commonly see animated gif images on web pages. Many of the **motion clips** available from the PowerPoint Motion Clip Gallery are animated gifs.

Animation

Animation simply means movement. You can add movement, or animation, to many of the **objects** that appear on a **slide**, including slide **text**.

Animation scheme

An **animation** scheme is a preset collection of animation effects you can apply to **slides**.

Applets

Applets are essentially miniature programs that are built into the larger PowerPoint program. PowerPoint supplies several applets, including Microsoft **Graph** and the Microsoft **Organization Chart** applets.

Audio track

A song or part of a song from a music CD that is played when a **slide** is displayed.

AutoContent Wizard

The AutoContent Wizard displays dialog boxes that ask about the **presentation** you want to create. Based on your answers, the wizard creates a rough-draft version of the presentation.

Bulleted list

A bulleted list is the list of **text**, or bullet points, that appear on a **slide** underneath the slide title. Bulleted lists can also be numbered, in which case they're not bulleted lists but rather numbered lists.

Chart

A chart is a picture that shows quantitative information. Pie charts, line charts, bar charts, and column charts are all examples of charts. In PowerPoint, you can create charts using Microsoft **Graph**.

Clip Gallery

The Clip Gallery is a tool you use to find and then place on **slides** the **sound clips** and **motion clips** that come with PowerPoint.

Color scheme

A color scheme is a set of eight compatible colors that PowerPoint uses for the parts of the **slides** in a **presentation**.

Custom slide show

A custom **slide show** is just a list, or subset, of **slides** you want to display as a separate, customized **presentation**.

Data category

Data categories organize the **data values** in the **data series**. On any **chart** that shows how data values change over time, the data category is time, which means that the data category names will be time-period identifiers: years, quarters, months, or some other time interval.

Data series

Data series identify the information you're plotting on a **chart**. If you ask the question "What does my chart show?," every one-word answer generally identifies a data series.

Data value

A data value is the number, or numeric value, that Microsoft **Graph** uses to create bars, columns, or lines that visually represent the data on a **chart**.

Design template

A design template provides a **color scheme** that is used for all the **presentation's** slides; a title **master slide**, which shows how your title **slide** looks; a slide master slide, which shows how the non-title slides in your presentation look; and a set of auto layouts.

Drawn objects

A drawn **object** is an object you draw using the PowerPoint drawing tools.

Graph

Graph is an **applet**, or small program, that you use to create **charts** for your **slides**.

Handouts

Handouts are printed copies of your slides that you hand out either before your **presentation** so that people can take notes or after your presentation so that people have a record of what you said.

Kiosk

You can set up a **slide show** to be delivered using an unattended computer—or what's known as a kiosk **presentation**. With a kiosk presentation, PowerPoint automatically advances from slide to slide based on rehearsal timing data.

Master slide

A master slide, essentially, is just a blueprint for creating individual **slides**.

Meeting Minder

The Meeting Minder lets you keep minutes or notes of a **presentation** meeting. You can also use it to record action items or to-do list items that stem from the presentation and meeting.

Motion clip

A motion clip is a movie, video, or **animation** file placed on a **slide** and played when the slide is displayed.

Objects

Objects are tables, **charts**, and pictures you place on a **slide** to augment any **text**. You can create a rich variety of useful objects using the PowerPoint program. You can also create objects using other programs like those that make up Microsoft Office. In fact, anything you can create or store on your computer can probably be turned into an object and then placed on a PowerPoint slide.

Online meeting

In an online meeting, you give a PowerPoint **presentation** on multiple computers connected to a network and then use an electronic whiteboard to collect comments from the meeting participants.

Organization Chart

Organization Chart is an **applet** or small program you use to create organizational **charts** for your **slides**.

Outline

An outline is just a list of the **slides** in your **presentation**. An outline includes both the slide titles and, if it exists, any bulleted text.

Pack And Go Wizard

The Pack And Go Wizard creates a stand-alone version of a **presentation** that includes all the **slides** in your presentation and a PowerPoint browser program that lets you show these slides. You use the wizard to create a copy of a presentation you can show on a computer that doesn't have the PowerPoint program installed.

Picture

A picture is a photograph or other graphical image stored in a file. You can add a picture to a **slide** by using the Clip Gallery.

Placeholders

Placeholders amount to boxes, or areas, you use to affix **objects** or **text** to a **slide**.

PowerPoint

PowerPoint is a **presentation** program. That means, in a nutshell, that it helps you create **slides** and then helps you show those slides to audiences. PowerPoint is also part of the Microsoft Office suite of programs.

PowerPoint program window

The PowerPoint program window shows the usual title bar, menu bar, and one or more toolbars. In the area beneath the menu bar and toolbars, PowerPoint displays a **presentation** window.

PowerPoint Viewer

If you create a stand-alone **presentation** using the Pack And Go Wizard, you use the separate PowerPoint Viewer program to deliver your presentation.

Presentation

A presentation consists of the **slides** you've both created and stored in the same file on your computer. A presentation is also, from the PowerPoint perspective, a document file.

Presentation broadcast

In a presentation broadcast, you deliver a **presentation** over a network. PowerPoint comes with the tools and software you need in order to deliver a presentation broadcast to as many as 15 people over a network.

Presentation window

A presentation window is the portion of the screen used to display the **presentation** you've opened or are creating.

Rehearsal Timing tool

When you're rehearsing your **presentation**, the Rehearsal Timing tool provides timers that show the time you've spent on a **slide** and on the presentation. You can use the timing information collected by using this tool to automatically advance through the slides in a presentation.

Slide

A slide is the basic building block you create using PowerPoint. If you were giving a slide show using, for example, a 35mm slide projector, a slide is displayed on a screen or wall.

Slide layouts

Slide layouts are simply blank **slides** that include **placeholders** for things like **text** and other **objects**. When you select a slide layout, simply pick one that shows the object placeholder or placeholders you want.

Slide show

A slide show consists of the **slides** you want to present to an audience. A slide show might include all slides in a **presentation** or consist of some subset of the slides in a presentation.

Slide Sorter

The Slide Sorter is a **view** that displays small pictures of each of the slides in your **presentation**. You use the Slide Sorter to verify that both the slides and their order are correct.

Slide transitions

Normally, PowerPoint simply displays the **next** slide in a **presentation** so that no noticeable transition occurs between slides. You can specify, however, that PowerPoint use a slide-to-slide transition that makes the change from one slide to the next slide noticeable. For example, you can tell PowerPoint that the current slide should be wiped away to review the next slide underneath.

Sound clip

A sound clip is a sound file placed on a **slide** and played when the slide is displayed.

Speaker's notes

Speaker's notes are notes or comments you want to use as you talk about the displayed slide. The Normal **view** provides a Speaker's Notes pane you can use to enter and store these notes.

Special effects

Special effects are garnishments (like **slide transitions, animation,** sound, and video) that you add to a **presentation** to enhance your presentation's impact and value.

Table

A table is a grid of columns and rows. The cells that make up the table—a cell is the intersection of a column and row—can contain **text,** number values, or even pictures, thereby making them powerful tools for organizing information, especially quantitative information, like financial data.

Task pane

The panel of the PowerPoint windows that provides hyperlinks and buttons you can click to choose common commands.

Text

Text represents the basic building block and the most common element you'll use on your **slides**. Text is used to label slides, and it can also appear in **tables** and in **bulleted lists**.

View

A view is just a way of looking at some of the information in a PowerPoint **presentation**. One way to look at that information is by looking at the **slide** and nothing else. This method is called Slide Show view.

Web presentation

If you have a web server, you can publish a PowerPoint **presentation** to a web site. After you do this, anyone with the ability to view that web site can view the **slides** in your presentation. After the presentation has been published to the web site, the PowerPoint slides become, in essence, web pages.

WordArt

WordArt is an **applet,** or small program, that you use to turn chunks of text into colorful, interesting graphical **objects** for your **slides**.

Index

animating text, 101–2
as building blocks, 2, 5, 13
changing, 77–92
defined, 5, 218
first, adding, 23
hiding, 119
moving in Outline view, 36
moving in Slide Sorter view, 119
numbering, 95
rearranging in Outline view, 36
rearranging in Slide Sorter view, 119
relationship to master slide, 77, 86
summary, 37
titles for, 24
title slides, 74
too much information on, 27
transition between, 97–100, 119
Slide Show Help dialog box, 150–51
slide shows
    boosting speed, 133
    custom, 129–31, 148
    defined, 151, 218
    looping, 132, 156
    vs. presentations, 151
    rehearsing, 125–28
    running through to review, 119–20
    running with PowerPoint, 146–51
    running with PowerPoint Viewer, 152–54
    selecting slides for, 130, 133
    setting up, 131–33
    stopping, 154, 155
Slide Show view, 9
Slide Sorter view, 9–10, 98, 117, 118–19, 218
slide transitions, 97–100, 119, 218
Slide Transition task pane, 98–99
sound clips
    adding to presentations, 108–12
    controlling timing, 110
    glossary definition, 219
    as part of slide transition, 100
    playing, 109
    playing music CD tracks, 116

selecting from Clip Gallery, 108–11
sound files as, 110–12
Sound Recorder program, 112
spacing lines, 92
speaker's notes
    displaying during presentations, 149
    drafting, 121–22
    glossary definition, 219
    planning, 122–23
    printing, 124–25
    reviewing, 124–25
    tips for creating, 122–23
    writing for ease of reading, 123–24
special effects. *See also* animation; movie clips, adding to slides; sound clips
    glossary definition, 219
    transitions between slides, 97–100, 119
spell-checking presentations, 37–38, 205, 206
splitting table cells, 47
spreadsheets. *See* Microsoft Excel
status bar, 193
stock charts, 175–76
stopping slide shows, 154, 155
Style Options dialog box, 206–8
summary slides, 37
surface charts, 172–74

T

tables. *See also* data tables
    adding rows or columns, 46
    adding to charts, 62–63
    adding to slides, 41–43
    changing background color, 47
    cutting and pasting in, 44
    filling with information, 43–44
    formatting, 46–48
    formatting borders, 46–47
    glossary definition, 219
    moving, 45–46
    positioning, 45–46
    resizing, 44–45

Tables And Borders toolbar, 46–48
task panes
    Custom Animation task pane, 102–8, 114
    defined, 9, 219
    Insert Clip Art task pane, 49, 109
    New Presentation task pane, 10–11, 16, 74, 192
    Slide Design task pane, 21, 83
    Slide Layout task pane, 22, 193
    Slide Transition task pane, 98–99
templates. *See* design templates
text
    aligning in placeholders, 88
    aligning in tables, 48
    anchoring in text objects, 94
    animating, 101–2
    centering, 40, 88
    changing case, 88–89
    changing font, 86–87
    copying, 33–34
    defined, 5, 219
    deleting, 33
    editing, 33, 199–201
    formatting, 86–92
    justifying, 88
    left-aligning, 88
    limiting, 27
    line spacing, 92
    moving, 33–34
    right-aligning, 88
    selecting, 33
text boxes, formatting text in, 94
35mm slides, 136–37
time, adding to slides, 95
time-series charts, 56, 162, 163
timing, presentation rehearsals, 125–26, 133
title master slide, 74
titles
    animating, 101–2
    for chart axes, 60
    for charts, 60
    for presentations, 18, 19, 20, 24
    for slides, 24

title slides, 74
toolbars
    customizing, 209–10
    Drawing toolbar, 70–71
    Formatting toolbar, 95–96
    Outlining toolbar, 34–37
    Picture toolbar, 52–53
    showing/hiding, 34
    Tables And Borders toolbar, 46–48
    WordArt, 184–89
transition between slides, 97–100, 119
transparencies, color, 135–36. *See also* 35mm slides

U

underlining, 87
uppercase, 88–89

V

video clips, adding to slides, 112–14
viewer. *See* PowerPoint Viewer
views, 9–10, 219
Visual Basic for Applications, 212
voice, tips for presentations, 127–28

W

Web, delivering presentations via, 156–58, 220
web browsers, using to display slide shows, 154–55, 158–59
Web Options dialog box
    Browsers tab, 196
    Encoding tab, 198
    Files tab, 197
    Fonts tab, 199
    General tab, 195
    Pictures tab, 197–98
web pages
    customizing, 195–99
    publishing presentations to web sites, 156–58, 220
    text replacements for graphic images, 95
    viewing presentations as, 158–59

windows
    customizing, 192–93
    document, 9
    presentation, 9, 217
    program, 8–9
wizards
    AutoContent Wizard, 10–12, 15–20
    defined, 4
    Pack And Go Wizard, 139–41, 152, 153
WordArt, 71, 181–89, 220
World Wide Web. *See* web pages
wrapping text, 94

X

xy (scatter) charts, 169–71

Z

Zoom box, 119

The manuscript for this book was prepared and submitted to Redmond Technology Press in electronic form. Text files were prepared using Microsoft Word 2000. Pages were composed using PageMaker 6.5 for Windows, with text in Frutiger and Caslon. Composed files were delivered to the printer as electronic prepress files.

Interior Design

Stefan Knorr

Project Editors

Becky Whitney
Paula Thurman

Technical Editor / Layout

Minh-Tam S. Le

Indexer

Julie Kawabata